Praise for *The Good Daughter*

'An aching, longing book of hard-won truths. If you've
ever felt homesick no matter where you are, or floored
by grief and familial duty, let Kumi Taguchi and
her story be your companion.'
Benjamin Law

'At once so personal, yet utterly universal.
A visceral, thoughtful and emotionally compelling story.'
Melissa Leong

'Like the Japanese art of Kintsugi, Kumi weaves gold through
the pieces of her life – and her father's – binding every part
with empathy, compassion and understanding that will speak
to anyone who has struggled to understand their parent,
themselves and the world they live in.'
Amy Remeikis

'A tender and contemplative reflection of the guideposts that
have marked the life of one of Australia's premier long-form
interviewers. Kumi turns the lens on herself to examine her
family's kaleidoscopic multi-national heritage and choices
formed by circumstance, tragedy and resilience.'
Jeremy Fernandez

The Good
Daughter

The Good Daughter

Kumi Taguchi 田口久美

SCRIBNER

SCRIBNER

First published in Australia in 2025 by Scribner,
an imprint of Simon & Schuster (Australia) Pty Limited
Level 4, 32 York St, Sydney NSW 2000
New York Amsterdam/Antwerp London Toronto Sydney New Delhi
Visit our website at www.simonandschuster.com.au

SCRIBNER and design are registered trademarks of The Gale Group, Inc.,
used under licence by Simon & Schuster LLC.

10 9 8 7 6 5 4 3 2 1

A catalogue record for this
book is available from the
National Library of Australia

9781925750799 (paperback)
9781925750805 (ebook)

Cover design by Hazel Lam
Cover photographs: (Front) supplied by the author; (back) courtesy of SBS
Cover image: (flowers) Blad met strooipatroon van bloemen (1900–1985)
by Anonymous/Rawpixel
Internal photograph: Supplied by the author
Extract from 'Little Gidding', in *Four Quartets* by T.S. Eliot © Faber
Typeset by Midland Typesetters in 12.5/17.5 pt Adobe Garamond Pro
Printed and bound in Australia by Griffin Press

For The Girl in the Green Dress

We shall not cease from exploration
And the end of all our exploring
Will be to arrive where we started
And know the place for the first time.

T.S. Eliot

And men go abroad to admire the heights of mountains,
the mighty billows of the sea, the broad tides of rivers,
the compass of the ocean, and the circuits of the stars,
and pass themselves by.

Saint Augustine

Contents

Preface

I started writing this book six years ago. This is my third go. I threw out every single word of the first two drafts and started over.

In reality, I have been writing this on and off for most of my adult life. Sometimes jotting down moments, sometimes talking through thoughts with friends, sometimes just sitting by myself and trying to work some things out. Over the years, what became clear was that no amount of talking and thinking ever seemed to shift a deep feeling inside me that something was missing.

'What's the rock in your pocket?', my writing mentor asked me, when I told her I was stuck with my book. 'You know, that thing you just can't let go of, that question you keep coming back to.' The answer came immediately: 'I want to know why I feel so lost.' Then I felt teary and my chest ached and that was when I knew I had to keep writing.

I knew a few places to look: a feeling of displacement around my mixed heritage, a sense I was not quite like other people, a lack of confidence. There was shame in there, but I could not quite put my finger on why. And then there was my father. I did not grow up with him and did not know him well, but he was always going to be at the core of my story, for that is where the pain seemed to lie.

What I found in my exploring was that I would keep circling back to common themes, and the memories that felt the strongest, had similar hues. I would skip back and forth through time. Things I had forgotten would resurface and put their hand up as if to say, Hey, I need to be in this, too.

So I tell my story in the way I came to understand it: through fragments of my childhood, memories from adulthood, core moments of isolation and understanding. They swirl back and forth in this book, much like they do in our minds. Along the way, I slowly discover a father I hardly knew and in doing that, slowly get to know myself.

In the end, I discover that I'm not lost anymore: I am home.

Missing

Alexei

I met Alexei when I was 22 and I knew him for less than a day. He was tall and thin and had smiley blue eyes and held an umbrella over my head when it started to rain on a cold winter's day in Moscow. He was a handful of years younger than me and way too young to have scars on his face, but that's just how it was.

He spoke very few words of English and I spoke very few words of Russian – although, later in the car he turned around from the passenger seat and, with his smiley blue eyes and teeth that were too big for his mouth, spoke one sentence in Japanese – (Hello, how are you?). I told him I understood him, and that his accent was great.

I was on holidays and spending the day with my new friend Kim. I had met her on my first evening there – she was staying in the same apartment as me, sleeping on the floor. She told me she was more comfortable on the hard ground than in a bed.

She'd just come back from spending a few months in a refugee camp in Pakistan, sussing out a story, and had become used to sleeping that way.

Kim was now based in Moscow, spoke fluent Russian, and we bonded over a shared love of adventure and people and seeing the world. Just a few nights earlier, we had found ourselves in a restaurant on a side street in that magnetic city, joining a birthday party of people we didn't know, dancing to music we didn't know, and laughing so hard at the absurd moments that incrementally shape a life.

On my final day, Kim brought me to the outskirts of Moscow to watch the rescue service put on a display. She was researching the organisation for a story she was writing and asked me if I wanted to tag along. Of course, I said yes. It was an annual thing, a chance for volunteers to show off their skills in simulated emergencies: climbing ladders into burning buildings, ramming through locked doors to rescue people trapped inside. It was makeshift and innocent and we stood huddled together as the winter cold set in and made its way through our boots and numbed our toes.

Alexei was part of the show and was keen to look after us. He walked back and forth, from the field to us, from us to the field, checking to make sure we were OK. He brought us an umbrella when it started to drizzle, then later, paper cups full of hot tea when the freezing cold really set in. On each visit, I would notice something new about him. The belt around his waist was too long and was pulled past the final hole. In addition to the scar on his left cheek, there were scars on his hands. His face was too thin, his cheeks sallow.

Kim told me later that Alexei was still waiting to be paid from another job of his, with the army, so the work with the rescue service helped put bread on the table for his grandmother and him. What about the scars, I asked her. She said they were from the war, and when I asked which war, she told me of a war I knew little about. How could it be, I asked her, that this has happened to him when he is younger than me?

The hours moved along, and our feet got colder, and I checked my watch. I was due to get on a plane to London that night and started to calculate the drive back into the city. I still needed to pack my bag and get myself to the airport. I have to get going soon, I told Kim. I didn't want to, but the anxiety was beginning to set in.

Alexei and his friend offered to drive me to the airport, and reluctantly I said yes – even then, it felt indulgent to take them away from practising their rescues, from work that seemed more important. The friend was a doctor, older. He looked a bit like Mel Gibson and when we told him that, he laughed, and then we laughed, and from then on we called him Mel.

We all piled into his small white car – Mel driving, Alexei in the passenger seat, Kim and me in the back. Wedged in between the two front seats was a pile of cassette tapes. Mel popped an 80s mix into the stereo, and everyone smiled as it came on. Kim and I looked at each other and shared that glance, the one where you just know what the other is thinking: isn't this crazy and isn't this fun and look at this moment we are living in.

The memory of what happened next sits in my body like a physical presence – one that has shifted my cells, and that doesn't exist in the realm of words. I live it and feel it more than I can describe it. But I will try.

We were driving along, me and Alexei and Kim and Mel, smiling to the 80s music. I remember looking out at the grey rainy sky, and even though it was only mid-afternoon, the light was fading in that strange Northern Hemisphere way, sort of sideways and around, no real zenith. Car lights were already glowing red and white on the highway.

I was feeling very guilty by this stage. I was grappling with the fact that Alexei was skinny and hadn't been paid, and now I was mentally calculating the cost of the petrol for this long trip to the airport, via the apartment for my very important flight to London. And while it was Mel's car and maybe he could afford it, to me, this was all one big window into poverty. I felt spoilt and embarrassed.

I whispered to Kim my misgivings. Alexei and Mel didn't speak English and couldn't have understood us, but even so, I didn't want them to hear guilt in my tone. Kim said it was totally fine and that they wanted to help. We talked about how wrong it was that often those who have so little, give the most.

Then the traffic slowed. Alexei and Mel turned and said something to Kim who told me in English that there had been an accident ahead, and Alexei and Mel wanted to see if they could help. This was not a drill, this was for real. We said it was fine and Mel stopped the car. Alexei told us to stay put, and then he and Mel jumped out into the rain.

Kim and I were in sudden silence. We sat in the back seat, wiping the condensation from the windows, trying to see what was going on. The traffic was totally jammed and, while I was worried about whatever had happened ahead, I was also thinking about how I was never going to make my flight.

Through the clear circle I had made with my hand, what I saw made no sense. Car after car had been squashed into each other. One car stood out; it was at right angles to the traffic, and near it a motorbike lay on its side. I scanned further and saw a body lying on the ground. And then, further along from the body there was something else. I squinted and realised it was a leg that had belonged to the body and I felt like I was in some dream.

An ambulance came up suddenly behind us, but drove past the mash of cars and the motorbike and the body and the leg. Another came past but it too drove past the body and the leg. Alexei ran back to see us and said they wouldn't be too long. He explained that there had been other accidents so there were other people needing help, and the passing ambulances were full and unable to stop but hopefully the next one would have room. He apologised and said to me don't worry, we will get you to the airport in time.

Then he ran back to the body and I watched as he and Mel put a tarpaulin over it to keep it dry. We waited. After about 20 minutes finally an ambulance arrived that wasn't full. Alexei and Mel loaded the body into it and then went back for the leg and loaded that into the ambulance too. When they ran back to the car, Mel switched on the engine and the same 80s track came back on and they started singing along as if nothing had happened. It was then that I started to cry.

—

A week before I left Sydney for Moscow, I went to pick up a winter coat I had put on layby for my trip. The coat was black and long and had a hand-woven feel to it. It grazed my ankles. I thought it was elegant and grown up and had been paying it off in small instalments for months. I handed over the last $20, the black coat was handed to me and when I got it home, I felt overwhelmingly proud. It was mine. And it was coming with me on my first solo overseas trip.

I had bought an expensive suitcase, too, one that had wheels that turned both ways and, when you opened it, had a hook you could unfold, so the entire suitcase could be hung up like a portable wardrobe. I spent hours packing it and re-packing it, making a spot for my coat and for my toiletries and tucking photocopies of my passport and credit card into an inside pocket. On my last night at home, I packed it for the final time and hung it on the back of my bedroom door.

—

They thought I was crying because I was worried I would miss my flight. Which made it worse. No, I wanted to tell them. I am crying because I have been in a bubble and you are thin and you save people and you look after your grandmother and you offer us tea and hold an umbrella over our heads and you are driving me to the airport and I feel ashamed and I don't want to leave. But I left all of that unsaid. How could I explain to them, via Kim's Russian, when I couldn't even find the words to explain it to myself.

All I could do was tell Kim that it wasn't fair, and she said I get it, and I said I just want to save Alexei, take him home and give him food. And she said, that's not how it works but I know the feeling. I sat in my sadness until we got to the apartment and I packed my suitcase with wheels and they helped me carry it down the stairs. The wheels didn't work on the cobblestones so they cradled it instead, and I wished I had just bought a backpack, not a suitcase that had a hook so it could be hung on the back of a door.

Kim and I sat in the back seat again. Alexei folded my black coat that grazed my ankles and placed it on my lap and smiled. I started adding up how much I was worth. Suitcase, $350. Coat, $250. Flights, $2,000. How much food could that buy over here? I wondered what they thought when they carried my suitcase over the cobblestones. What did they think of me? Probably nothing, but my shame ran deep.

They drove me to the airport and in the rushed minutes I had left with them, Kim took a photo of us on my disposable camera – me in the middle, Alexei on my right with his arm around my shoulders, handsome Mel on my left, his posture certain. They were smiling, I was crying, still trying to process the umbrella and the tea and the body and the leg and the suitcase and the winter coat. I said goodbye and walked onto the plane and into a new kind of existence.

—

Before the accident, when I was in the thick of planning my trip, I had imagined a different London. That city had been the real destination, Russia an interesting stopover. I had written a list of things I wanted to buy: *fun pants from a market, chunky watch.* I wanted to hear music and see plays. The first night I arrived,

I had planned to meet my cousin at a barge on the River Thames. She was putting on a puppet show, and I was going straight there from the airport.

I stuck to that plan. My cousin was the only person I knew in London, and I was going to stay with her for a few nights. This was pre-mobile phones too, so even if I had wanted to change plans – 'had a bit of a strange thing happen in Moscow' – I couldn't. So I spent more money than I care to think of on a black taxi to the barge. There I found my cousin and had a glass of champagne and met her friends and chatted. But I wasn't really there. I was still at that frozen field with Kim and Alexei, I was still in Mel's car, I was still at the airport saying goodbye.

It felt stomach-sinking wrong to be chatting about whatever it was we were chatting about – the lights on the Thames, the show, the weather, the getting-to-know-you chat and 'how do you know so-and-so' – while I knew there was a skinny man with blue eyes in Moscow trying to put bread on his grandmother's table. One situation felt real and deeply human, the other unreal and distant, and I was in the wrong one.

Exhausted, I sat down on a bench underneath the barge window. I should have been looking out to the night lights of London. Instead, I hung my head and it was then that I saw my boots – they were still caked with mud from the frozen field in Moscow. My jeans had mud on the bottom of the legs. I was in one place and also in another and my clothes bore the evidence. It was a relief to see the dirt, to know it really had happened.

In the days that followed, I wandered around London in something of a daze, disconnected from everyone around me and all the things I had planned to do. I had no desire to shop or wander around museums. Instead, I sat in parks and drank coffee. I walked. I took a train to Oxford and looked at gargoyles on buildings. I filled in time.

After a few days, what I needed to do became clear. I emailed Kim and told her I was going to come back to Moscow. Kim told me she could help me get a visa, make it look like I was working for a furniture company or something. I was all in, I told her. I will move. I will learn Russian. We can make films together. *All I have to do*, I wrote to her, *is go back to Sydney, hand in my resignation, end my lease and pack my bags.*

It was all so doable. I had nothing tying me down, no responsibilities to anyone else. I was working an admin job at the youth radio station, Triple J. I spent my days booking flights and writing reports – not a dream job. The dream was to tell stories. In Moscow I had found what it felt like to be truly alive, to be connected to real life and real people and real struggles – and I wanted more of it.

When I got back to Sydney a month later, everything felt different. My friends, in turn, said there was something different about me – perhaps it was knowing that I was heading somewhere else, that I *was* somewhere else. I had changed. But that certainty, that tone in my email to Kim, started to shift, too. On my first day back at work, I didn't resign. Nor did I on the day after that, or the day after that. And after a few weeks, I was back into my routine and work was OK again and I didn't feel so different after all. Moscow started to feel very far away.

I made up excuses not to go: the timing wasn't right, I told myself that my career was going well, that everyone had to start somewhere. At least I was in media, at least I had some path ahead.

I had stability, I knew where my money was coming from. I wrote to Kim and said, *Not this time.* But even in my words to her, I could feel they were just excuses.

I developed the film from my camera and wound back time to what I had seen just a month earlier: St Basil's Cathedral and the Hermitage Museum, the outside of a gun shop, a street protest where everyone was wearing silver sequins, a homeless man sitting on a pavement, a woman in a camel-coloured winter coat outside an upmarket department store. A row of strollers at a park in St Petersburg, the inside of a cinema, blini at an underground café by the Neva River.

And the last photo in the roll: Alexei and Mel and me at Moscow's Sheremetyevo International Airport. The one taken in a hurry by Kim after our car trip to make my flight on time. And because of that rush, we didn't have time to reposition, so we were backlit. I could barely make out our faces. I couldn't see Alexei's thin cheeks or blue eyes, I couldn't see Mel's smile and floppy hair, and I couldn't see my face, but I remember it was wet with tears.

And year after year following that one day in a wintry city, I would look back at that photo and know that this was the moment I promised myself something deep and true, and also that, soon after, I would abandon that dream. And abandon myself.

—

Perhaps I should have started from the beginning, when I was born and what house I lived in and where I went to school. My friends and fears and the moments I felt separate and the moments I felt whole. University and relationships and road trips and music that helped me imagine alternative lives. First jobs and first loves and first debts and my first solo run around the leafy streets of home number six – or was it seven or eight? – holding a portable CD player with rubber bands around the case, finding the perfect position so the music wouldn't skip.

But my memories don't go in a straight line – they swirl and go backwards and forwards and fold back in on each other as we continue to meet newer and older versions of ourselves. Once, I interviewed world-leading physicist Brian Greene about science and faith and whether a person could hold both to be true. Afterwards, off camera, I asked him if he could solve just one mystery, what would it be. He stared across the Brisbane River, thought for a few moments, looked back at me, and replied: Time. I would want to know what time really is.

So I am going to tell this story in a different way – one that doesn't pretend I have all the answers even about my own life. Instead, it's a way that might make sense to a 16-year-old me, who was also struggling with these questions and had an experience I still think about.

That summer, like a few before and after it, my family – being my mum and my sister and me – spent a few weeks in a ramshackle cottage near a beach hugged by tall cliffs. I had been given a cookbook for Christmas and it told me about Italy and villages and tomatoes ripened in the sun. I pored over photos of bread and fish and markets and women holding baskets in fields of olives. From that book, page 27, I started making focaccia. I would wake up before the sun, measure out the flour, add enough yeast and knead the dough just so; I formed it into a round ball and placed it in a bowl, brushing the top with olive oil and leaving it to rise under a damp tea towel. I'd go back to bed and then, a few hours later, get up again and flatten out the dough – fashioning it into a rectangle. The last stage was another lashing of oil, generous sprinkles of sea salt and sprigs of fresh rosemary. I'd pop it in the oven and have fresh bread waiting for the household when it woke.

There was something in the making that felt comforting: producing something, creating something made me feel grounded while mostly – for reasons I didn't understand – I felt quite lonely and sad. At night, as some sort of expression of that isolation, I would walk to the end of the street to the beach and feel my way through the grassy dunes and onto the cool sand. The first night, I wandered along the shore and listened to the waves and their night-time rhythm. The second night, I sat on the sand and dug my toes down. The third night, I lay on my back and looked up into the blackness. One star here, another there, they seemed to beckon.

As the minutes ticked by, the stars became brighter. And then there were more of them and even more still, until a blanket of light covered me and I felt small and safe and connected to a vastness I didn't understand but wanted to be part of. All that brightness from stars that no longer existed, but that still connected all the scattered souls looking up.

–

My Australian mum, Mary, taught Japanese to Aussie primary school students. Every year she would tell them – and me, for I was in her class, too – about Tanabata, a star festival. It's celebrated on the seventh day of the seventh month. That's when, according to a Chinese legend, two stars that are usually separated by the Milky Way are reunited. The legend goes that a weaver and a cow herder met and fell in love and got married straight away. But because their love was so deep, they forgot about their jobs. She stopped weaving and he stopped herding cows.

Her father got so angry that he forbade them from being together. His daughter begged him to let them stay in the sky among the stars. He finally agreed but said they could meet only once a year – on the seventh day of the seventh month. On that day, a flock of magpies came and built them a bridge, so they can walk across the river of stars. It is said the magpies won't come if it's raining, so on that day of that month, every year, the Japanese ask for clear skies so the lovers can meet.

The Japanese

The Japanese.

The first time I really heard that term was in Year 9 at high school. Up until then, I had described myself and my family as some form of 'Japanese', usually with a qualifying 'but'.

My dad is Japanese, but I was born here.

My dad is Japanese, but I don't see him much.

My mum teaches Japanese, but she is Australian.

I visit Japan, but I have never lived there.

My name is Japanese, but it's shortened; it really should be Kumiko, but my parents decided to make it Kumi so that it wasn't too Japanese.

But learning about *'the* Japanese' caught me by surprise.

We were studying modern history and had gone through the timeline of World War I and the Depression and then we got to World War II. We learned about Australia and America and England and Germany and Japan. And then we turned the page in our textbooks and there were photos of emaci-ated men, just skin and bones, who had been taken prisoner of war by the Japanese. They were tortured and enslaved and many died.

The Japanese did this.

It's a cliché to say silence can be deafening, but I felt it here from a teacher, a reply over there by a fellow student. But one page over, where the inhumanity of war was shown in black and white, the silence that came over the room wasn't just a lack of sound. It was a discomfort. And it took me a few moments to realise what was going on. The Japanese. Oh, is that me? Is that how people see me? Hang on, I thought we were all the same? And if it is me . . . should I say I'm sorry?

I can't remember much more about the lesson. I think we moved through the part about the Japanese quite quickly; it was swept under the carpet, and I swept it under the carpet too. But in that moment, I felt a separation open up between me and everyone else. And from then on, I carried around a shame that wasn't mine directly but felt like mine nonetheless.

—

In my early twenties, I lived on the other side of the country, in a region three hours south of Perth. My then boyfriend, Ben, and I had been there for a year, and had decided it was time to pack up and head back east.

I was anxious about what life would be like after this chapter was over. We'd had a great time together, but we were both escaping something. Now it felt like real life needed to begin, whatever real life was, and neither of us was sure whether we would start that together or apart. We didn't even know how to talk about it, so we talked about everything else instead.

In the days leading up our departure I found myself drawn skyward, looking up at the blanket of stars like I had as a teenager on summer holidays, taking comfort from the vastness.

One of the final things I did before we drove the thousands of kilometres across the desert was jump onto the NASA website. I had heard that there were new images from the Hubble Space Telescope, and NASA had made hundreds of them available. This was a revelation – I was blown away that I could get an image for free, download it and have it on my computer forever. And in the face of change, I wanted to be able to boot up my computer in a few months' time and see the same picture. A silent reassurance.

On our last night in our packed-up house, I spent a few hours scouring the website, looking for an image that spoke to me. I chose one that was bright and mysterious and enthralling – the Horsehead Nebula. The grey cloud reared so high and with such certainty. I tried to imagine how big it was and if I would ever be able to measure it in my mind, and I wondered whether it moved or whether it would always be the same shape.

I right-clicked and it downloaded, and I right-clicked again and made it my desktop picture. Then I took a deep breath and shut down the computer, knowing that when I saw the image again, my life would somehow be different.

We drove across dry red dirt. We stopped at the bottom of the continent and looked south towards Antarctica. We slept on a platform we had built inside the four-wheel drive. The headroom was so tight we could barely roll over in the night. One morning, after arriving at a campsite late the night before, we flung open the back doors to see that our view was the endless ocean.

We sat on milk crates on the side of highways to eat a basic sandwich, sometimes washed down with a plastic glass of cheap red wine for the passenger. After a few days, I was desperate for a salad and some fresh fruit. But we were on roads that stretched out straight for a thousand kilometres at a time, and on land that would evaporate a drop of rain before it even hit the ground, so food was limited to whatever an isolated road-house had in store. Usually something that had been frozen, of a potato variety.

Somewhere along this Nullarbor stretch, I decided I would go and see Dad. Since I'd last seen him, I had gone through high school and played hockey and softball and met other dads, who stood on the sidelines and told their daughters to run faster and that they were proud of them. I had played the violin in hundreds of concerts and made money at uni playing in quartets for weddings and in pit orchestras for musicals. I had waitressed in a Mexican restaurant that was famous for hosting hen's nights where an inevitable penis cake was the finale. I had cleaned ashtrays in bars and watched as a husband came in at 11 am and dragged his wife out by her hair, declaring that she had wasted all his money on gambling. I had got my driver's licence and had driven from Brisbane to Sydney a number of times to see the first Test cricket match of the season. I had rented flats and nearly been kicked out of flats because the parties were too loud. I had made friends and lost friends and had landed my first job in the media. In the ten years since I had seen my dad, my world had changed.

Dad had come up in conversation with Ben over the years. Mainly, in the form of me complaining. *He was never around. He was a hopeless father.* Whatever the issue, I was always angry, and the conclusion was always the same: I didn't need him. And I didn't need to see him again. I had even forgotten that he was a journalist, too. I couldn't – or didn't want to – see any positive connections between this distant man and me.

Ben thought differently. While driving one of those endless stretches where there's nowhere to stop and nowhere to hide, he gave me a bit of a talking-to. You need to deal with this father thing, he said. We were stopping in Melbourne anyway, where my dad lived, so why not see him. I felt uncomfortably exposed, like he had detected this big flaw in me that I was oblivious to – or even proud of. I felt hurt and defensive, I twisted and turned. But underneath, I knew he was right. I asked him to come with me; he said this was something I had to do on my own.

We had very different views on why I should see my dad, though. Ben thought I needed to repair the relationship to get over this angry/absent father thing. I wanted to see Dad one last time so that I could close the door on that part of my life. I didn't even need to tell him that. I just needed to confirm for myself what I already knew: that I didn't need him. And more than that: I was better off without him.

—

My Australian granny loved gardening, amongst many other things. She told me once about a plant that used to grow in the desert in South Australia. It was from the aloe family. Hardy survivors with juicy stems, aloes can grow almost anywhere, even in dirt devoid of nutrients and as dry as dry can be. She told me that wild animals love that plant. They had eaten it for generations, until the plant disappeared for a few years. When it reappeared, it was different: the same roots and stems and the same juicy insides, but the stems were now covered with small, evenly spaced thorns. Spiky and impenetrable. *Good luck getting to me*, that plant was saying. *I am protected now.*

Eventually, though, the animals found another way to eat what they needed. They worked their way through the thorns, adjusting their mouths around the spikes – similar to how a horse nibbles at a purple thistle flower: expertly avoiding the thorns, gently pressing its lips towards nourishment.

Hybrid Blood

I was born two months early in a hospital in Melbourne and spent the first month of my life in a humidicrib. Controlled visits and controlled sounds and controlled temperature. I imagine it would have felt safe in there, secure and consistent and knowable. All the things I would later come to value and crave.

On top of my humidicrib sat a little toy called Piglet, though I am not sure when he was named or who named him. He was made out of navy-blue corduroy. His tummy was embroidered with flowers, and he had red silk inside his ears. He was my first toy and first friend and for years he came with me, from this new house to that new house, sometimes in my bed, sometimes on my desk, and as I got older, propped on a dresser.

I was born early because about ten years earlier, my mum had fallen in love with Japan. She visited on a whim – a holiday before taking up a job as a teacher in Sydney – and ended up staying for nine years. She went back home to pack a suitcase and quit the job that was meant to start her adult life. (I know. While I only thought about it, she actually *did* it.)

In the early days, she lived at the side of a monastery in Kyoto. She would often regale me with stories of how little money she had and how she used to eat yakitori, chicken on sticks, from a place underneath a bridge near a train track, the cheapest she could find. One day when she told newfound friends about her food hack, they replied that people said the meat served there wasn't chicken but cat. No matter how often I heard it, that story horrified me each time.

A few years into her Japan stint, my mum got sick (not from the not-chicken-but-cat sticks). She collapsed and when the ambulance came, they realised she needed a blood transfusion. They asked her whether she had normal blood. She said, 'Yes', because at home her blood type was the most common.

What she didn't know, though, was that in Japan her normal blood was not their normal blood. The transfusion scrambled her system – it didn't kill her, but it did make having children dangerous. The first pregnancy would probably be fine, the doctors explained, because her body wouldn't really register that there was a foreign object growing inside her. But, by the second, her body might try to attack this foreign object.

I was the second.

And the doctors were right. When Mum was about six months pregnant, her body saw me as a threat and started attacking me. She was given two options:

1. Give me full blood transfusions in utero, which could kill one or both of us, or

2. Give birth to me way too early, hope that I survive and do the transfusions on the outside.

24

She chose the latter, and that's why I was born in November, not January, and why I weighed just over a kilogram, and why a silent, safe humidicrib with a navy-blue Piglet on the top was my first home.

Mum told me that one day when she was coming to visit me in the hospital, she got in a lift and overheard a couple of doctors chatting to each other. They spoke about this preemie baby, a girl, and how she was Eurasian and how it was a miracle this baby survived and one of them said: Yes, she has two things on her side. One, she is a girl. And two, she has hybrid blood.

—

Ben told me once, perhaps when we were driving across the red dirt roads, that plants from different species that were grafted with each other were the strongest. I don't feel like that, I replied.

—

A guy who thought he was being funny once called me a mongrel, and I guess that's another word for hybrid. It was around the same time a movie came out called *The Adventures of Priscilla, Queen of the Desert*. In it, there's a scene where an Asian woman does a striptease in a pub and puts a ping-pong ball up her vagina and then shoots it out. The crowd hollers. It was funny, apparently, and the scene everyone talked about.

Another guy, who, after asking what I was and me telling him I was half Japanese, looked me up and down. After a while, he rested his eyes on my groin and said, I know which half is Japanese.

One time, I was waitressing at a wedding in a vineyard three hours south of Perth and I was asked to serve food to the guests at the bottom of the garden. There were trays of cheese and crackers, some prawns and chicken on sticks, little pancakes with fish roe on them, and plates of sushi with soy sauce and wasabi on the side.

I happened to pick up a tray of sushi and made my way to a group of middle-aged men. I felt sorry for them. As a consummate snacker, at any event I deliberately place myself where the food is coming out or hang near the catering tables. These guys were at the wrong end of the party and were never going to get fed unless I went to them.

I weaved my way through pretty dresses and white smiles and floral perfumes, balancing the tray on my upturned hand. I found them, laughing and chatting with half-filled glasses of beer.

Would you like some sushi? I asked them.

They stopped talking, and one of them looked at me and looked at me again, and said, Nah, we don't eat that shit. We killed them Japs in the war.

Another time, I was standing in the courtyard of my then-home with another ex. He was, and still is, a bit older than me. We were hosting a party and chatting to a guest, who told us about her art gallery. The conversation between the three of us bounced back and forth, seamlessly.

But then, quite abruptly, she turned to him and whispered, as if I was suddenly not there: You're lucky, they don't age. *They.*

And another time, I had moved back to Sydney after spending six years in Hong Kong and was starting over again, finding work and doing the hustle, meeting managers in newsrooms and sending my CV to anyone I could find. I was shown to a corner office and went through the usual chit-chat – what I had been doing and what I wanted to do. I did most of the talking, and after about ten minutes, there was nothing coming back to me. The man opposite me sat still, with his arms crossed.

'The thing is,' he told me, 'audiences want to see people who look like them, and that isn't you.'

There was silence. Nowhere else to go with that, really. So, instead of the usual polite wrap-up where they usually say 'we'll contact you if anything comes up', I said to him, Maybe I should go now. And he said, Yes, that sounds good. So I stood, and he kept sitting down, and I showed myself out. I called a friend from outside the building and told him what had happened. He told me they were idiots and not to be upset and that I wasn't for them anyway. I said, Yeah true, but underneath I wanted them to want me, to pick me, to choose me. Don't worry about it, he said. Then he had a laugh and I had a laugh, but I didn't find it funny. Apparently, we laugh when we feel hurt or uncomfortable. A survival thing, I guess.

And this one (now I'm backtracking quite a few years) when I was working in a record store in Sydney, starting a new life in a big city. A man with angry eyes and an angry spirit made his way towards me. I spotted him from the front of the store and could see him working his way through the aisles, his gaze fixed on me.

When he finally got to my counter, he leaned over and stared at me and eventually spoke.

'What are you?' he asked.

'Me? What do you mean?' I replied.

'I said, what *are* you?' he repeated, agitated.

I knew what he wanted to hear. I am half this, half that, blah blah. But damn it, I wasn't in the mood for explaining myself that day. So I mustered up the courage and looked into his dark eyes and said:

'I'm a human. What are you?'

—

After my month in survival mode in the humidicrib I went home in time for Christmas. I cried a lot – all the time. I wasn't really formed. My lungs were tiny and my body hadn't had time to do all the things it needed to do, to become all the things it needed to become.

I was needy, apparently. Ever since, I've hated that term. I've hated that I was small and that I cried. Later, I was told I wasn't a good hugger; I told myself that was because my first month was without hugs and my body learned to do life on its own. But, deep down, I felt like a failure. Like I was somehow flawed from the beginning. I feared I'd never get better, never *be* better.

As I went through my twenties and thirties, I felt increasingly like I just couldn't do life like everyone else. Somehow they had it all together and I was constantly flailing. One night, I googled something along the lines of: the emotional development of a premature baby. I wish I hadn't. *Could have difficulty managing emotions, could have problems coping, might have lower self-esteem, are more likely to have anxiety or depression later in life.*

I went down a rabbit hole. I read books on brain development and knew how vital those first three years were, embedding all those pathways in the brain. I watched the *Seven Up!* documentary from 1964, where the filmmakers followed a group of people and caught up with them every seven years – at seven, then 14, then 21, and so on. The premise was this: 'show me a child at seven, and I will show you the man'. Basically, who you are at seven will fundamentally be who you are at 49, or 56. One character stood out to me. A quiet boy who, in the first episode, was asked what he wanted to be when he grew up. He had no idea and, in a quiet voice that matched his soft spirit, he said: 'I just want to see what I can see'. And then, was it when they found him at 35, he was still childlike, still a bit lost. Things in his life hadn't really worked out. Apart from his body changing, his mind and spirit were the same. I already had some idea that I was needy and underdeveloped, and here was the science to back it up.

And I thought, *I am fucked*.

What's in a Name?

I spoke to Tim for only an hour, ten years ago, but a few times a year I wonder whether he's still alive. I'm not sure why I remember him, or why I'm meant to remember him, but I do. I was writing a story on people who had gone to war as one person and come back another. For two weeks, I spent long days at the Heidelberg Repatriation Hospital in Melbourne, being a fly on the wall, taking notes and observing art therapy classes and sitting in the canteen when inpatients ate their lunch. The idea was to get them to trust that I was there for the right reasons – to understand, not to exploit – and hopefully have a few agree to tell me their stories.

Tim decided to talk to me towards the end of my second week there. He said at the outset that he was only doing it because he wanted people to understand. He didn't want to share, he didn't particularly want to be in a room with me, but he felt it was a duty to talk.

We sat across from each other in a small carpeted office on what felt like school chairs. He barely made eye contact, his voice barely went up or down, nor did it speed up or slow down. It was all the same. He was just – present.

I remember the facts. Now in his mid-thirties, he signed up with the army at 17 and was selected to join the elite of the elite. He was trained beyond what most of us would ever know or understand, to do things most of us will never have to do. He rarely went a day without perfectly cropped hair and a clean-shaven face.

And I remember him saying that at 29, he began to lose his mind. And how at 30, he became unable to function and was back living with his parents, and was in and out of the rehab hospital – the sort that is meant to reshape your mind and your person and your place in the world – for the best part of five years.

Now he lived on a remote property with only trees and silence for company. He went to the supermarket once a month. (Although the word he used was 'mission'. As in, I go on a mission to the supermarket once a month.) Apart from his psychs, he spoke to two people – his mum and his therapist. In the same tone of voice, he told me he had tried to kill himself five times and felt like a failure because he couldn't even get that right.

His hair was now uncut – not long, just not tended to. He wore a cap, the peak pulled low, so I could barely see his eyes. His face was covered with a beard, his torso draped in a loose-fitting T-shirt. His tracksuit pants were too big, too loose. As he spoke, I tried to imagine the man he had described, the one with the perfect hair and clean face. He would have stood tall, his body lean in a tailored uniform for a tailored life. Now he struggled to even get out of bed.

I asked if he could describe what his world felt like. Try to imagine being crushed between two opposing forces, he told me – one is grief, the other rage. That's what it is.

You don't come across as angry, I replied. I am just being polite to you, he said. I am angry. And then he said, I am sad. And then he said, I am so, so lonely.

I didn't know how to respond. I wanted to tell him I was sorry and that everything would be OK and I wanted to help him, but I knew there was nothing I could do. I don't want sympathy, he told me. But do you know why I don't cut my hair and why my beard is messy? Because maybe then people will see me and know that I am not OK.

I didn't want to say goodbye. I didn't want him to go back to his property, with only trees and silence for company. But he left and went back to his life, and I left and went back to mine. And now, every few months, I wonder how he is doing, but really, what I want to know is whether he is living, or just living as a dead person, or whether he is truly dead.

I don't know how to find him. His name was never Tim. He asked to be anonymous, so at the beginning I told him he could choose whatever name he wanted. The smallest smile came across his face (it was a nice smile, a hint of who he was):

You know that Captain from the TV show *Blackadder*? The funny one? he said.

Oh, you mean Captain Darling?

Yeah, that's him. I could be him.

Then he paused, and he smiled a bit again, and I smiled back, and he said: Yeah, maybe not. I think I'll just go with Tim.

—

In the 2001 Japanese animation film *Spirited Away,* a young girl named Chihiro gets caught in a spirit world and is given a new name by the old woman for whom she ends up working. As she is given this new name, Sen, her old name floats off on a piece of paper and her new friend Haku, who can't remember what he was called, tells her that if she forgets her real name, she will never be able to return home.

—

In Japan, when people ask you your name, they ask you what your kanji are – the pictorial characters that the Japanese adopted from the Chinese. My name, Kumi, could be written in a variety of ways, depending on what kanji are chosen. There is not one character for 'ku', and not one character for 'mi'. So, I might meet another Kumi, and our names will sound the same – but the meaning of our names might be different.

Maybe because they didn't know whether I would survive my early birth, my parents chose the character meaning 'forever' for 'ku', and the character meaning 'beautiful' for 'mi'. Forever beautiful. I have always felt awkward about the meaning and have never really owned it. An elegy that accidentally turned into a burden.

—

After Dad died, I found a piece of paper among what remained. My name in kanji, written by him (and I was surprised that

I recognised it was his hand). It looks beautiful, scribbled in pencil.

And below that, again written in English, what he saw as its definition: true, peaceful.

—

My sister was born two and a bit years before me, in Tokyo. Outside Mum's hospital room was a tree, hardy and green. My sister was named after it. Maki. Her kanji, 'true' and 'precious'.

We laugh even now at her arrival, because it was on the exact day she was due. Yep – *Here I am, world, bang on time.* And that is how she has always been. Firm, unwavering, certain.

Unlike me, she was able to leave assignments to the last minute. She'd never stress. She'd do an all-nighter and ace them all. Me, I was always preparing way too early and over-thinking every step.

Also, unlike me, she never saw her hybrid blood as anything to be ashamed of.

Genes, hey. Same, same, but different.

—

We had a shortlist of names for my daughter, before she was born. Ella and Jasmine were there. A few more that I can't remember. And, at the bottom of the list, Coco. I'm not sure where I got that from but it seemed like a possibility.

One day, a work colleague came to visit. She had two kids and seemingly knew what parenting was all about. She came with bags of children's clothes she no longer needed and asked me whether we had chosen a name yet. I said no. She replied:

your child will choose its own name. What bollocks, I thought, but I nodded and smiled.

Anyway, when my daughter was born, I decided to introduce myself to her. Hi Ella, I said, to her little perfect face. Hi Jasmine. I ran through the other names and then got to Coco. Hi Coco, I said to her big brown eyes.

And that was it. She was Coco. Her face said it, her eyes, her demeanour. Somehow, that name just worked.

Years later, when she was about six, my daughter told me she didn't like her name, and wanted to change it. I told her she was welcome to, and then proceeded to explain a legal process and deed poll and how she needed to wait until she was 18.

And then I said to her: the thing is, you chose your own name.

—

Japanese people don't have middle names, but at school I got sick of saying I didn't have one, so I made one up. I decided my middle name would be Erica, because one year in one of the groups of students my mum took to Japan, there was a girl called Erica – I liked her long red hair, and she seemed cool.

After a while I started to believe in my own invention, so when I said Erica was my middle name, I didn't think I was being totally untruthful. And it felt nice to be a bit more normal.

My first name was bad enough. People would respond, 'What? What is it? Connie? Katie?' At times, I wondered what it would be like to not have to explain your name, spell it, laugh with others when they thought it was funny or strange.

And my eyes. If I wore sunglasses, for a while I was like everyone else. I could hide the biggest giveaway, the one that was the cause for mockery. I noticed that guys looked at me the way they looked at the other girls. And it was not just in my head. On the days I didn't have my sunnies on, I am sure the conversations were shorter, there was less interest.

Contrasting that were the men whose dating history was only Asian women. The ones who liked to use words like 'exotic', like they had somehow earned a prize.

Around the same time we all laughed at the part in *Priscilla* where the Asian dancer pops ping-pong balls out of her vagina, a certain politician whose name I would prefer not be in this book, decided all these Asians coming to Australia were taking everyone else's jobs. There was an election on and it was my first time voting. When I turned up at the polling station, there were people handing out pamphlets telling you how to vote to make sure no more Asians came into the country, and a banner was slung between two trees – AGAINST ASIAN MIGRATION.

–

I was talking to a friend about all this one day. I was in my mid-twenties and we were wandering through sunny Sydney on a weekend morning, as was our routine. We'd get a coffee and read the paper and chat about life. On this day, I was feeling down. I told him how I wished I had been born blonde and how everything would be so different and – I remember this moment so clearly – I was pressing the button at a pedestrian crossing, waiting for the traffic to stop – and he said to me: Maybe it's got nothing to do with that. Maybe people just don't like who you are.

I was quite shocked. I felt confronted and small. I had always thought of myself as a nice person, hard-working and thoughtful.

Interested in people. Curious. I had my insecurities, yes, but in general, I felt as though I was liked. In a split second, my mind raced to all these other possibilities and, instead of pushing back or even telling this friend how I felt – wow, that hurt – I just accepted what he said as truth.

And that maybe I had been using my Japanese-ness as an excuse, a 'this-is-why-the-world-is-shit' trump card, and not looked at other parts of me that might need some examining. By the time we reached the other side of the road, I had decided that if he was sick of hearing excuses, maybe everyone was – and that it was up to me to stop making excuses too.

So, I tried even harder to be better. And on the days I wished for blonde hair or blue eyes, I would tell myself not to be a victim and that other people had it worse than me. But underneath, I felt hollow and ashamed and lesser and I kept it all to myself because no-one wants to hear how lost and isolated some of us might feel.

But many years after that pedestrian crossing and the vagina movie and the 'let's get rid of Asians' votes – that is, many years after I'd decided 'not to make too much of it' – I was told I had missed out on a job because I was 'too risky' and that they had gone for the safe option instead. And in that moment I knew it was about my eyes and my name and I remembered the father of my friend who said they didn't buy Japanese cars and the wedding guests who didn't eat sushi because we killed those Japs in the war. Who was meant to have moved on? I felt my older self and younger self meet – I was both exhausted and naïve – but somehow also each comforted the other.

Hello, Horsehead Nebula

The last time I had seen my dad was when I was about 12. My sister and I visited him in Melbourne for our annual holiday. Each year, he would prepare an itinerary for us. Movies one day, Puffing Billy train the next. Sometimes we even went to the zoo. On this trip, he decided to take us to Tasmania. The plan involved driving to the ferry terminal, putting the car on the ferry, getting the car off the ferry, then driving around the small island.

Pretty early, things started to go south. Dad never spent extra money, so when all the other families went to the ferry café and got hot chips for lunch, we ate pre-made onigiri, rice balls, covered in seaweed. Dad had wrapped them tightly in plastic boxes, securing the lids with crisscrossed rubber bands. I remember sitting in an isolated area of the deck, holding my onigiri and wishing I just had a normal family, a normal dad.

From there, I have a spattering of memories, all negative. The strange way he drove, turning the engine off when we went downhill to save petrol, then switching it back on at the bottom of the hill so we could climb again. The way he put the gears in neutral as much as he could. I even hated our itinerary-allocated 'Free Time'. Allocated time didn't feel free.

We called Mum from a payphone about halfway through the trip. I want to come home, I said. I missed my cat and my bed and I was stuck on an island with a dad I didn't know. You have to get through, Mum told us. We told her we were malnourished and only eating rice balls, and we just wanted some sausages and meat. We weren't malnourished, we just felt alone. And vulnerable.

We did get through the rest of the trip. We found a few op shops one day and we watched *Point Break* in a small cinema. I felt normal for the first time in a long time. We found snippets of fun amid what felt like duty. But now I can see that deep down, what it really felt like was guilt. Guilt that I was not being a good daughter. Guilt that I was not being grateful. Fear that Dad would think less of me.

I don't remember saying goodbye. I would have said thank you, but just to be polite. I don't remember the trip back home. But when I finally got back to my cat and my bed, I decided that I never wanted to see my dad again. Decision made. Armour on.

—

The home I went back to was my favourite of all, in a small country town between Sydney and Canberra. Our house was white and wooden, with a long concrete verandah at the back. My room had double doors that opened up onto a big pine tree. I got to choose the fabric for my curtains, which Mum made.

I chose a calico with small camels and people in rows, a pattern that repeated all the way down.

In my room was a single bed and a small desk, made from a painted unused door resting on two white cabinets. My desk lamp doubled as a bed light. I loved my room. I would often go to bed, thinking about how to rearrange it and then, with the puzzle sorted in my head, I would get up at midnight and start dragging my furniture around. I loved the fact that in a few short hours, in the quiet of night with crickets chirping outside, I could change so much, and feel so different, just by rearranging things I already had.

The house was on 15 acres of land, and we had a mini farm. Our cats, Jezebel (mine), Humphrey (my sister's); our dog, Maud (Mum's); then horses, Sophie, Sunny and Caspian. We had chooks, too, called Hazel, Esther, Lorna and Primrose (making up the acronym HELP. Though when Primrose died, and we adopted another called Charlotte, the acronym fell over.) We had ducks, too. We thought they were the same gender until they ended up having ducklings.

Sometimes, when our horses got sick with colic, we would get up in the night, pull our boots on, and walk them around and around to stop them from lying down, waiting for the vet to come. In winter, we would carry around large, empty hessian horse-feed bags and pick up pinecones for our fireplace and wooden stove, and kindling to get the fires going.

My favourite memories were of food. Mum made Japanese food but in a robust Aussie way. Instead of a few pieces of karaage, fried chicken, we had piles of it, all hot and crunchy in big ceramic bowls. And instead of a neat row of gyoza, fried dumplings, she made an endless supply. We'd have friends around, all sitting at a long wooden table with antique wooden benches as seats. Mum made square cushions out of Japanese fabrics, to mark where we sat.

She might have fallen out of love with Dad, but not with Japan – she just managed to blend Japan with Australia. So much so that when people asked me which parent was Japanese, I would always hesitate. Because my Japanese way of living came from my Aussie mum, my brain always took a beat to reconcile where my Japanese-ness, at least in terms of my genes, came from. My dad, I would eventually say. My dad is Japanese.

Later, when I would look back at that kitchen and that food, I would see this wonderful, bizarre blend of everything whole-some: a small farm and animals, boots at the back door, turned upside down so spiders didn't get in, an open fireplace and stars forever. And then, noren, the Japanese curtains that hang down in doorways, white paper lights, low cushions to sit on the floor around our coffee table, piles of Japanese food and pickles and sauces. This was a form of hybrid that worked.

–

And now, a decade or so later, after crossing the Nullarbor, I was looking for my dad so I could say goodbye. Not a 'goodbye Dad', just a silent acknowledgement within myself, that I had seen him and, yep, he was not for me.

I got his address somehow. It was somewhere new, in the outer suburbs of Melbourne. He had moved to a retirement village the moment he turned 55, and started another chapter of his life. There, he was the young buck on the block. He did the

Sunday sausage sizzles and helped the older residents with their shopping bags. They loved him and called him Aki, easier to say than Akira. That was how Dad introduced himself. I am Aki, he would say.

Getting off the tram, I found my way to his home, winding my way up small roads through the retirement village, where every house would have been identical were it not for a couple of small personal touches – a gnome on one doorstep, pansies in a pot on another, wind chimes hanging from someone else's garage, different doormats.

At Dad's house, Unit 142, I raised my hand to knock on the door. Then I lowered it, wanting to turn back. What was I doing here? I had nothing to say. But I sensed he knew I was there already, and I was right. I had barely knocked when the door opened and there he was. My dad. He looked familiar. I knew him. I felt unnerved, like a chunk of my armour was being pierced with familiarity.

Hi Dad, I said. Hi san Kumi, he replied. I gave him an awkward hug and told him he had a nice house and asked him how he was. My voice sounded higher, more eager to please. He told me to come in, and made a cup of tea with hot water from a flask. He told me he boiled the kettle only once, in the morning, using the hot water from the flask for the rest of the day.

We ate senbei, Japanese rice crackers, and he wanted me to eat a mandarin. It is good for your health, he said. I ate it, even though I didn't want to. We quickly ran out of things to say to each other. Then he asked me whether I wanted to see his new computer.

Dad had always loved technology and showing me and my sister his gadgets. A shortwave radio he'd had for decades and used to listen to broadcasts from the Pacific. A tape recorder. Headphones. And later, after one of just three visits back to Japan in the 44 years he lived in Australia, he showed us a new electronic typewriter he had bought, which could write in both English and Japanese.

I told him I would love to see his computer, although inside I was groaning. Here we go again, I thought, the same show-and-tell. But I just had to go through the motions, then I could leave and go back to my life.

We walked down a tiny corridor to his bedroom. There was a single bed, partly made, with his dressing gown laid on the top. A small wardrobe and a simple desk. Pens in a container, a few notebooks, some newspaper clippings. (Did I tell you he was a journalist? I know. I *know*.)

He sat down at his desk and pulled a plastic cover off the monitor – he looked after his possessions so well – and he leaned down and switched on his new gadget. While the computer was starting up, he told me how he could email his nephew in Japan and look things up on the internet, and even print off articles in Japanese.

That's great, I told him, counting down the minutes until I could leave without being rude. *All I'm doing here*, I kept telling myself, *is seeing all the things I do not like about my dad*. That way I could, with evidence, walk away and never need to come back. Daughter duty done.

The computer finally came to life and as the monitor lit up, I noticed a familiar image on his desktop. I moved a little closer and looked over his shoulder. I had seen it just a few weeks earlier, as I'd packed up my computer on the other side of the country.

I had picked it out of hundreds of others and downloaded it to my desktop.

As it turns out, Dad had done the same.

There was my Horsehead Nebula, vibrant and alive.

Immediately, I felt something in me soften; a hardness shifted, and it was replaced by sorrow, a sorrow that would take me years to understand.

That this man, with his thinning hair and comb-over, his hard-to-understand English, was like me and I was like him and I felt an ache for intangible things, for parts of myself I didn't realise I had lost. And I knew, too, that the door I was intending to close had just been thrown wide open.

Sara

'Do you like coffee?' With this simple question, Sara and I became friends.

We met during our first few days of university: I moved into a residential college and Sara was in the room next door. At first glance we could scarcely have been more different – I turned up in jeans, with a violin slung around my shoulder; Sara was in a shiny matching tracksuit, her hair in a sporty ponytail. We probably said hello that first day, but were swept away with everything so new and unknown and exciting all at once. A few days later, we ran into each other in the corridor and started chatting. Before too long, we were sitting together, drinking coffee, and from that day on, Sara was in my life and I was in hers.

We lived in that college for a year, then moved out together into a flat, and the following year into another flat with another friend. We were still so different yet so the same, too. Her speciality was sport and exercise science; mine, music and creativity.

But I was sporty in my own way, and she was interested in music and movies and art. In the Venn diagram of our different lives and interests, there was enough intersection to contain a lot of wonderful things. Some days, I would hang out with her sporty friends, their legs shaved for this triathlon or that bike ride. Other times, Sara would come to an exhibition I was in, or a concert. Our lives crisscrossed and wove into each other, and have done so ever since.

When we left uni, Sara decided to travel for nearly a year: working at pubs in London, camping and trekking through Africa. How will we survive, we asked each other before she left. This was pre-mobiles, pre being able to message someone from anywhere in the world, any time. But our friendship did survive, in handwritten letters sent across the seas. We would write to each other every day, a small, *Hi, you won't guess what happened today*, or a scribbled thought on the back of a beer coaster. And then maybe after a week or two, we would send off a huge wad of our lives to the other, sometimes with a dictaphone tape inside so we could hear each other's voices.

In Sara, I found other ways to look at life, as hard as that often was. While I was always stewing over how to make things better, how to be better, Sara was much more accepting of life. Instead of spending an eternity grappling with something, she'd tell me, matter-of-factly: 'Well, the timing just isn't right.' I wanted things to be right, and right now. And that often stopped me from living from a place of trust.

An example: after moving back to Sydney from Hong Kong after six years away, I started dipping my toes into the dating pool. A picnic here, a dinner there. Funny stories and crazy stories.

Some I laughed at, others I didn't. What was clear, though, was that none of these guys were into anything long term. No commitment vibes. If I had mentioned this to any of my other friends, they would have said the same thing: typical men, why can't they ever commit, story of my life, etc. But not Sara. She looked at me and said, genuinely curious and without judgement: I wonder what part of you is attracting men like that?

Damn, I thought. *What if she's right?* And then, *Crap: if she is, I have some work to do.*

After a particularly bad break-up, when I was grieving and cleaning up in its wake, Sara said to me one day: look for signs. 'Signs of what?' I asked her. Signs in nature or animals or anything unusual. They sometimes help us to understand; they help us see that there is something bigger going on. I told her I would look, though clocking that wasn't *I* meant to be the Eastern, Zen philosopher in this friendship?

In the weeks after, a flock of white cockatoos would sit outside my window, high up in the canopy of the trees. They were associated with new beginnings, I found out. There was a scrappy one with grey feathers, and he would sit looking at me. *What are you trying to tell me*, I would ask him. Another day, a black crow flew back and forth in the sky. Transformation, change and freedom, I learned.

We look for signs, something to help us try to understand our world. For me, my Horsehead Nebula moment with Dad was something. A random coincidence, sure. But I chose to believe it was more than that.

Missing People

I was five when my parents separated and about seven when I ran away from home. I told my mum and my sister that I was never coming back. I am not sure what happened and I didn't actually want to run away, but I did want them to care that I was going to. I slammed the front door and pretended I was off, but in reality I snuck down the side of the house and crouched behind the rubbish bins.

I sat there for what seemed like ages. I waited for them to come out the front door and call my name, but they never did. I could hear them chatting away in the kitchen. Laughing, even. I waited longer, expecting them to be worried. Hoping they would be worried. After all, it was getting close to dinner time. But they didn't come looking for me. My knees got sore, and the light started to fade, and I waited a bit longer.

Eventually, I went back inside. I wanted them to say that they were worried about me and missed me and were so glad

I was home safe. I wanted them to say sorry, for something, anything.

But they knew I wouldn't really run away, and now I knew it too.

Then the question I really wanted to ask was: how did you know?

—

If I did go missing in Australia today, my name would end up on the National Missing Persons Coordination Centre, or the NMPCC. Long-term missing persons are listed alphabetically by their surname. At the time of writing, alphabetically I would sit between Melony Sutton and Martyn Tann.

Melony and her brother Chad went missing on 23 November 1992, the day before my 17th birthday. She was 14 and he was 16. They missed the bus to school, so they decided to walk. Later it was found that they didn't go to school and decided to hitchhike to the other side of the country. They were never seen again.

Martyn Tann was 25 when he was last seen near a beach in Western Australia. He was visiting from interstate and decided to hitchhike north. Rescuers searched the land and the sea but found only his backpack, close to where he was last seen. He would be in his mid-30s now.

I wonder what my three-sentence blurb would have said? There would be a few facts about how old I was when I went missing, what I was wearing, my age and height. Then, perhaps the last sentence would be this: *Last seen looking for home.*

—

The Japanese word jōhatsu means 'evaporation'. But the word is used to describe people, mainly men, who disappear without a trace. Dissipated. Up to 100,000 a year: one day there, the next day gone. The thing is, they haven't gone missing because of something sinister or untoward or evil. They've decided to make themselves disappear. They've lost their jobs or they can't conquer an addiction; they're depressed or they've strayed from their marriage. Whatever reason, it is to do with shame. And a shedding of one life, to start another.

—

The etymology of the English word 'disappear' can be traced back to the 15th century. Dis-appear. Do the opposite of appear. So, something that ceases to be visible, vanishes from sight, is no longer seen.

I guess it doesn't mean that thing is gone forever. We just can't see it.

—

When my daughter was five her best friend was a boy called Clark, and one day she came home from kindergarten and told me how only she and Clark saw fairies and no-one else did. And instead of feeling like they were the odd ones out, she thought the rest of the class was strange.

Do adults see fairies? she asked.

Not often, I told her.

Why not? her little voice replied.

Because they forget to look for them.

Scott

Scott was listed as missing for four days but I knew he was dead. The last thing anyone knew about him was that he was in a taxi with his mates on the way to a nightclub in Bali. A bomb had gone off inside the nightclub at 11:05 pm, and another outside the nightclub seconds later, where Scott was in a taxi. It was all but guaranteed that he was one of the hundreds who died.

Every day, the names of the dead were printed in the newspapers, and another list of those still missing. I would buy the paper each morning and scan the surnames listed alphabetically for Scott's, hoping it would stay in the missing column, but feeling it was inevitable that he would forever remain in one of the two.

Scott's dad flew over to Bali, and I heard that he visited morgue after morgue, looking for his son's body. Eventually – gradually – it became clear the taxi we now knew Scott was in had been so close to the force of the blast that there was not going to be a body. So one day his name did move from the missing column to the dead column.

It shook me more than it should have. I had met Scott only once, but even before I met him, he filled a room. His parents were friends with my family, and we had dinner with them often. Over my teenage years and over their dining room table, there was always a story about Scott, even though Scott himself was always elsewhere: Scott riding his bike to uni; Scott organising a dress-up party; Scott on the beach. He had such love for life and his sisters and his girlfriend – the woman who would later become his wife and later still, the mother of his only child.

The first, only and last time I met Scott was in my final year of high school. We had our obligatory careers day where various speakers come and tell you about life after school, and what we could do and who we might become. You could sign up for learning about law, or hear an ex-student talk about her path to medicine, or learn about life on a university campus.

I had no clear vocation in mind. I was just curious about the world, I enjoyed learning and I played the violin. For a few years, my music teacher had been pestering me about a creative arts degree at a university that was not well known at the time – the University of Wollongong. It would really suit you, she told me. I could audition and even though they took only 12 musicians, if I got through, I could have all my music lessons paid for and still do English and anything else I wanted.

I wasn't interested. The uni itself felt like a risk – it was relatively new, the degree itself was really new, and most people at my school went to more prestigious places and studied better things. Plus, I would have to audition and I was nowhere near good enough and they only took one violinist. The excuses ran hot. I kept telling her I wasn't sure, but I knew within myself that it meant no – although she was so certain about this path for me and I didn't want to let her down.

So, come careers day, when I scanned the list of sessions, I saw one for that university and I thought, *Maybe I'll just go*. And then I saw the name of the person who was going to talk to us – Scott. I thought I may as well go, even just to say hi and *I know your parents*.

So I put my name down, which wasn't necessary as there were only three of us there in the end, but that didn't seem to bother Scott. He was there waiting and could have been talking to a room of a thousand people. He stood at the front and his zest for life emanated from him, his eyes and smile beaming across the room. He spoke with unbridled enthusiasm about the uni and a campus that had a mountain as its backdrop and green lawns and ducks that roamed there. And he told us about the residential colleges and the uni bar and the band nights and the beaches and every word seemed genuine and full of a life I had never even considered. And after the 40 minutes ended, I knew I had to go there because I wanted just a sprinkle of what he had.

And so my series of nos became my deepest hope, and I went to the uni open day and saw the green lawns and ducks for myself, and met lecturers who might become mine, and saw the performance space and the soundproof practice rooms, and I could see myself there and the whole place just felt right. And on the way home that day, instead of feeling elated, I felt a deep grief of wanting something so badly it was already lost. My chances were so slim.

A few months later, after hours upon hours of practice, that teacher who said to me, this would be perfect for you, the one I had said no to many times over, drove me to the campus again. She would play the piano for me and the two of us sat together outside the performance space, waiting for my turn. She looked as nervous as I felt. Every few minutes, I'd wipe my sweaty hands on my uniform. I always used to sweat before a performance – the worst thing because my fingers would slip.

While we were waiting, I could hear the person before me in her audition. She sounded amazing. In this music world, there were people like me – hard workers, the six hours a day kind of musician, who had some ability but nothing incredibly special; and there were people like her. Just in her tone, her agility, her command of the bow – you can *hear* when someone is just that notch above. I wanted to leave.

While she was still playing and before I went in, her mother came up to me and asked how many other places I was auditioning for. Already feeling inadequate, I told her, just this one. Oh, she said, *only* this one? And I said, yes, just here, this is where I want to go. And she proceeded to tell me how this place was *really* quite far down the list for *them* – her daughter was aiming for, you know, the *established* places and they were just ticking the box, really.

And then she told me good luck, and I shrank a bit more, but before I could turn around and leave, my name was called. My music teacher smiled at me and said, You will be fine, and we went in together, and I wiped my hands one more time on my uniform, and I said hello and I started to play. Knowing that this one piece, and then a few musical tests after that, could determine my future. Just me, my violin and my teacher, who drove me all this way, the one who would leave Mozart chocolates in my violin case for me to find after an exam, the one who had said, this would suit you. It was her I was really playing for in that room. I wanted her to be proud of me. And it was my way of saying thank you.

While I was playing I also thought of my Aussie grandmother, who would come to every concert, dressing in her best clothes, often topped with her red woollen coat and a brooch – sometimes a cat, other times a flower. Her hair would always be in a neat low bun. I watched her do her hair sometimes, just from the doorway on my way past: a few bobby pins in her mouth, sitting at her dresser, her hairbrush neatly placed in front of the mirror.

Lastly, I thought of the man who was, for a handful of years, the equivalent of a stepdad. He lived with us and he mixed clay and he made pots, and on our small farm he had a kiln. Sometimes when I came home from school, he would tell me that the kiln was firing. He would let me look through the special viewing hole in the front, into the searing orange glow.

Once, when he came back from a trip to China, he knocked on my bedroom door – the only time I remember him coming into my room – and gave me a small stone horse. I said thank you and gave him an awkward hug and I sat it on my dresser and loved how it felt cool and heavy in my hands. And I thought of the time I came back from school and Mum told me how he had collapsed while playing sport and that he was in the hospital and then, maybe the next day, when I was told he wasn't going to live and asked did I want to go and say goodbye, I said no.

On the day of his funeral I told my friends I was going to the dentist because they all seemed to have real mums and real dads and somehow I felt ashamed that my family was different.

I went to the funeral, and I cried, and then I got back to school by lunchtime and when my friends asked how the dentist was, I said it was fine. Many years later, one friend told me she knew where I was that day and she asked me why didn't I just say. I told her I didn't know. I still don't. Maybe it was that feeling of experiencing something different to everyone else and not knowing how to talk about it.

That's what I thought about when I was playing for that one spot in a degree I just had to be part of at a campus I needed to have as mine and I knew I only had one chance, and when I went back a few months later as that one violinist who had been picked from among all the others, my first lesson was in that same hall and I met the same people who were now going to be my lecturers and I asked them, 'Why did you choose me when I wasn't the best?'

And they said, you had the most potential, and you played with feeling. And I thought, maybe being the best isn't the only thing. Maybe feeling our way through the world can be an asset too. And so began my life of playing and late-night orchestra rehearsals and sitting on the green lawns with the ducks roaming around, and trips to the beach and drunken nights that ended when the sun came up and later, when people would ask me what uni was like, I would say that going there was the best decision of my life, and I would tell them about Scott and how much he loved life, and I would tell them about his memorial service, which was held in the biggest lecture hall on the campus and how so many people turned up, there wasn't enough room, so they spilled down the stairs and crammed into the aisles and craned their heads around the doors.

And how, on the big screen, there was a slideshow of photos. Scott as a baby and Scott with his younger sisters and Scott with his wife and Scott at the beach and Scott at dress-up parties. And of Scott with his baby girl, who was not even one year old when he died.

Searching

The Violinist

For most of my school life, I was known as the girl who played the violin. I started playing when I was five. My instrument then was a tissue box with a wooden ruler as the fingerboard. I was tiny and my fingers were tiny. I never knew why I played. I just did it because that is what Mum chose for me and I happily accepted the brief. Music was important to her and it became my second language.

The tissue box became a quarter-sized real instrument and then it became a half-size and by the time I was about ten, I had a full-sized violin. I was good, not naturally great, but I put in the hours, and when I got to high school I came to like the solitude and the discipline. In a sound-proof room, I could go through my practice routine and that would give me a sense of calm and control over a life that felt uncertain.

And I could travel back in time. A page of Bach would take me to the 1700s, and a page of Mozart to a similar era, and as my eyes read the black notes that had originally been written by quill, quietly telling my fingers where to go next in an unconscious process, I let my mind go back to when the composers were alive. I imagined them sitting over parchment and hearing in their heads angels singing and violins dancing with violas, and I wondered whether they had ever pictured just how many hundreds of years their music would travel. I wondered how many people before me had played their creations, dot after dot, note after note.

I would think the same about writing. How amazing it was that just 26 letters in the English alphabet could open entire worlds to me: how a letter placed here and another there, a word in this order in a sentence, in that order in a paragraph, could shape my mind and my emotions and my dreams. I would pore over perfectly written sentences and wonder about the brain that was able to master those words in a way no-one else had, in that sequence, in that sentiment – what was it in their souls which allowed that to happen. I always saw that genius as pain. As sorrow. That mastery never seemed to come from joy. No, those feelings came from a person who had lived loss and sadness – and their way to understand the world was to put parts of it together in dots and notes and letters and words, and somehow those black marks on paper connect us to what it is to be human.

Humanity was what I could feel when I played the violin and it became important to me – a conduit to connect me to my inner world and feelings I could not express. I liked the discipline, too: if I put in the work, I would see a result – a simple transaction in a life that often felt complicated. Practise, get better, keep practising, keep getting better. And there was something else

I learned that would come to serve me, and also become an Achilles heel: I became a performer.

I started to play in orchestras when I was about 12, and that's when the performances began too. Recitals at school where I would stand in front of an audience and test my hours of practice – done in wonderful solitude behind closed doors – in front of hundreds of pairs of eyes. I would prepare a piece for weeks and then my name would be typed into a home-made program, and then it would be my turn. I would walk onto the stage and my pianist would walk with me, and they would sit down at the piano and I would stand straight and raise my violin and feel my hands get sweaty and my heart rate rise, and then, when I was ready to go, I would nod at my pianist and we would begin.

I was always worried about making a mistake. If you do make a mistake, I was told over and over again, just keep going. No matter what, don't stop. I had seen what happens when a performance goes off track. One mistake then turns into two and the embarrassment compounds; I had seen kids like me freeze and stop playing and cry and run off the stage. But somehow I managed to keep inside me all the stress and all the mistakes and all the embarrassment when my finger hit the wrong note, or when my bow flew off the strings, and I would keep going and I would make it to the end.

And when I finished, instead of the 95 percent of all that I had done right, I would remember the five percent I had done wrong. The way the opening note sounded a bit scratchy. The fumble at the start of the difficult sequence. The notes missed in the section I knew I should have practised more, but stupidly thought I would be able to wing it on the day. And I remembered my face going red and the feeling of being exposed and I wondered whether the applause at the end was real or whether we were all just playing the same game. It was so hard not to apologise after a mistake, but I wasn't allowed to do that either. After I finished, I would bow and say thank you and I would walk off the stage.

And so this cycle – performing and wondering what else I could have done better, performing and letting others down, performing and letting myself down – became my pattern. And no matter how hard I practised, I would always stumble and only remember what I could have done better. This repetition became wired in my brain and became an automatic way of being – in my violin life and in my real life. Later on, when I returned from a job interview or a date or an event, I would often lie in bed and scroll back through what had happened, and my brain would remember the five percent of things I could have done better. The thoughts kept circling and the message was persistent: *Just keep going, don't stop no matter how hard it gets, no matter how shit it feels. Smile and keep going.*

—

When I was 14, I wanted to know more about the world, and I decided I would find out through watching documentaries and learning about other people and how they lived their lives. At that time, I watched two documentaries, sitting in our house on the farm. They showed me worlds that were so remote and alluring: one was about people white-water rafting down the Himalayan rapids, where one man got stuck underwater for too many minutes and barely made it out alive; the other followed tribal hunters in Indonesia who hunted their prey by shooting poisoned darts from hollowed-out bamboo with just their breath. For my birthday that year, I asked Mum for a subscription to *National Geographic*. Every month, the magazine with its distinct yellow cover would arrive in a brown-paper sleeve at our farmhouse. The days when I would come home from school and find it sitting on my bed were my favourite. The worlds I visited in those pages felt more real and magnetic than anything I could have imagined for myself. I read every article numerous times. I interrogated every photo and checked the credits to see who had taken it, and wondered who they were and how they got to where they did. I wanted to be part of it. I wanted to be the one telling those stories. And as I went deeper into these worlds, what I became interested in changed.

At first, I was fascinated by the animals and the nomadic people and the tribes walking lands. But quite quickly I was drawn to war and poverty and hurt and injustice – I found a strange solace in the things that were darker and harder to understand. As if those experiences held some mysterious answers to the meaning of life. The more I felt for the world, the more alive I felt in myself, and the more these stories seemed to awaken in me the desire to connect with others. That perhaps in sadness and loss and grief lay deeper answers. That in the bleakest times, hearts opened and love could flow where it was previously thought impossible. That at the edges of loss were compassion and care.

I also became obsessed with spies and serial killers and saved up money to buy issues of the morbid *Murder Casebook* magazine series. Each edition focused on one person or incident: Jack the

Ripper, for example, or the John F. Kennedy assassination. I read them over and over into the night and went over every detail, bodies in bags and severed heads, and I would wonder how it could be that we are all born as babies, yet we can be so vastly different. The idea that another human just like me could quite calmly dispose of a life both horrified and fascinated me.

And I saw my future in a desert, a dusty land somewhere far from our little farm with chickens and ducks and horses. The Iraq War was on the news every night, and that is where I saw myself. I decided I wanted to be a war correspondent, and I would get back from school and change into boots and pretend I was in a nameless place on the other side of the world, reporting some form of the truth to everyone back home. I would walk along and address a pretend camera, talking about a war I knew little about, but I would make myself keep speaking, like they did, their hands in front, their eyes looking forwards. At first, I could only speak for a handful of seconds, then I progressed to half a minute, then a minute. Sometimes, I spoke about a pretend war. Other times, a car crash or a sporting event. Sometimes just about what dinner I was having that night. Any topic was fine, as long as I didn't stop. Just keep going, don't stop. I knew that well from playing the violin.

–

Sydney Opera House, 20 October 2018. The opening ceremony of the Invictus Games, a championship for injured servicemen and women – 500 competitors proving their worth in 13 sports. The ceremony was going to be watched by 60 million people around the world and I was one of the hosts. It was the biggest live show I had ever done and the security was insane. Prince Harry was going to be there to officially launch the games and Meghan was going to be with him. When he came in for his rehearsal, the entire site was locked down and we were told to stay in our demountables. Barely visible snipers positioned on the very top of the tallest iconic sail scanned the crowds below.

I was nervous and excited, and had to tell my brain I deserved to be here, because there had been doubters. People would ask, 'So, how did *you* get this gig?', then make a comment about diversity. And I would want to say, Well, you know all that work I have done on veterans over the years and on people who come back from war zones physically intact but mentally damaged? You know Tim the veteran, the man who hides behind his cap and beard? The one who calls a trip to the supermarket a mission? That's why. I care about what happens to these people. But I couldn't be bothered to explain, and I would think of that Aldous Huxley quote: 'Several excuses are always less convincing than one.' So I would say, 'They asked me.' Which was true.

The opening ceremony was scheduled to start at 7.30 pm. That afternoon, a huge electrical storm swept across New South Wales, one of the worst in decades. Around 300,000 lightning strikes hit the state, and a man was killed near Dubbo, 400 kilometres west of Sydney, when a freak lightning bolt smashed down to earth. By then, we were all locked down on-site and in major preparation mode – I was already getting my hair and make-up done in my demountable – but there was an underlying tension that was not just show nerves: we knew the storm was on its way to us. We hoped, somehow, that the predictions it would hit us just when the broadcast was due to start were incorrect and the storm would bypass us. It didn't. There were rumours of the ceremony being cancelled. Then we heard of some competitors breaking down in tears, for the games were what had kept them going. Something to aim for, an event to be part of, for their sacrifices to be acknowledged and celebrated.

The ceremony has to go ahead, I said to our crew. We have to do this.

I was halfway through getting ready when there was a knock on my demountable dressing-room door, a member of the crew telling us we had to evacuate the site. The storm was electrically charged and we were all in metal boxes, using metal stairs; our stage was metal, the equipment, sound desks, lights. Everything was a magnet for what was to come.

I grabbed my script, water and snacks, my make-up artist threw a few essentials in a bag, and we ran up to the Opera House where we were taken to a room at the back. We had no idea what was going on or whether the event was going ahead but we pressed forwards, as if it was. I watched out the window across the harbour as the storm bore down. The sky was thick and black, aggressive. The rain was pounding in sideways and thunder clapped overhead. I kept thinking of the snipers I had seen on top of the Opera House earlier in the day and asked someone about them. They'll still be up there, they replied. I was scared for them and I became worried for us. It seemed like a very real possibility that the ceremony might not go ahead. This wasn't a normal storm, this was a weather event, and although it didn't last long, only around half an hour, the clean-up was huge.

The ceremony was going to be postponed by an hour, and that's if all the checks were successful. This wasn't just a matter of wiping off a few raindrops and going ahead. All the electrical equipment had to be checked. Every surface, every step and ramp had to be dried. At broadcast HQ, schedulers frantically searched for programs to fill in the airtime.

Even under the best conditions, for me, live events have always been about battery levels. How do I keep my body fuelled, not only with food and water, but with enough energy in the tank to do the job? Let's say I am on at 9 pm, on a stage in front of the Opera House. That morning, I have woken up, already having planned what time to have breakfast because I want to plan lunch too, and make sure I time an early dinner without it being too early or too late.

I am also taking into account what I will be wearing and how I will eat and not spill on my dress. And, I will be taking phone calls and replying to last-minute emails, going through my script, saying hello to dozens of people, small conversations here and there. And every single interaction drains a tiny bit of that battery. So, it is impossible to be at 100 percent, by the time 9 pm rolls around.

That is when adrenaline kicks in, and the fear of failure. I might go on stage with 70 percent in the tank, but the remainder is made up of nerves and fear and excitement. Muscle memory helps, too. My brain and body just know what to do. I have come to trust that I will be able to make it through, no matter what.

On that night, I needed everything I had ever learned. We finally got on stage. The sky had cleared and the air was cool, and I was acutely aware of how close we came to not having a broadcast at all. It all kicked off well and the crowd seemed happy and relieved. My eye kept catching a competitor in the front row – sitting next to him was his assistance dog, loyal and sturdy.

After the first few minutes of delivering my lines and hitting my marks on the stage, I was feeling good. Your body knows when it is safe and I felt like it was all going to be OK. Then, it came to the first musical act. I introduced them and they walked out on stage, got behind their keyboards and synthesisers and . . . nothing. No sound. The storm had shorted all their equipment.

There was that horrid blank air, only seconds but it felt like minutes. And then, in my earpiece, the director's voice: *Kumi, there's something up on autocue, read that and we will play out a package.*

So I moved back onto the stage and made a comment about why the music couldn't happen right now and then read the words on the autocue and waited for this story to play out and . . . nothing. Major technical difficulties. Bear in mind, too, this is the public broadcaster so there are no advertisements. There is nothing to go to when it all falls over. So, I was standing there, and then I heard the words we in the industry all know and dread: *Fill.*

In media terms, that means ad lib until we can get this sorted. Make stuff up. Say anything. *Fuck*, I thought. With what? I wanted to say that out loud, 'Um, fill with what?' But I couldn't. I was the host, the one who needed to appear like I had it all together.

In my mind, I was thinking I would need to cover for about 30 seconds – ample time in TV land for the team to sort out what to do next. So I talked about the event and how many people were in the crowd and the storm, and I paused every now and then, giving my director space to say something to me like: *Great, that's enough. Or, yep, we got it sorted, you can wrap.*

But, with each pause, nothing. I looked up at the autocue, hoping it would give me some guidance But, black and blank.

A few more seconds of silence and then: *Kumi, keep going.*

Fuck, I thought again. And then for a split second I allowed myself to close my eyes and I saw my bookshelf at home. Rows of books about war: *Yellow Birds* by Kevin Powers, *War* by Sebastian Junger. *All Quiet on the Western Front.* Roméo Dallaire's *Shake Hands with the Devil. The Good Soldiers* by David Finkel.

And James Nachtwey's excruciating photography book, *Inferno.* A book I told my daughter not to look at until she was 18. I let her read anything and everything but that – that was off limits. *There are things in there that are very hard to see, and when you see them, you can't unsee them.*

At one point I thought, *Well, if this is how my career ends, it's not the worst of things.* But I snapped my head out of that and, using the muscle memory of years of performing – violin and news and reporting – I knew there was only one thing I needed to do: don't stop, just keep going.

And, in that instant, I remembered why I wanted to be here in the first place. A snapshot of everything I had been interested in became the fuel for a long (in TV time) fill. A few minutes of ad-libbing and this time I owned it: I talked about my bookshelf and all that had been written about war. And all that had been written by those who came back but came back changed. And I spoke about art and photography, all created from the same place: this is who we were, this is what we went through and this is who we are now.

A Garden in Tokyo

There is a building in the centre of Tokyo that has been a part of my life for as long as I can remember. Although I have changed, it has not. Same address, same carpet, same smell, same bed linen, same logo, same umbrella stands outside, same buffet breakfast.

It's a hotel of sorts, but you have to be a member to book in. It's charmingly daggy and simple. The lobby feels more like a library, with newspaper stands and small tables. To the left, a modest café which becomes a breakfast room in the mornings, then turns into a lunch spot, and in the afternoon, there is a daily cake special, with tea or coffee.

The café overlooks the most beautiful garden, which changes its personality as the spring buds turn to summer flowers, green leaves turn to autumn reds and the grass dries in winter. Couples get married in the garden, and some mornings, you can watch as they stand in among the green, their guests positioned a polite distance away, photographers respectfully milling around.

The rooms are small, most with single, built-in beds with a clock in the wood panelling. Each room has a built-in desk. The bathrooms are so tiny it's hard to turn around. The rooms are cleaned every day, and you know it because the beds are perfectly made and on the pillow a card has been placed, with the next day's weather filled out by hand. Yes, we know you can check the weather on your phone, it says, but here, we do things like we did before.

There is no gym, no bar, no happy hour. But there is a library full of books with leather-bound covers, older than the building itself, and rows of journals from around the world, their beckoning covers faced out. In that room, floor-to-ceiling windows frame a cherry blossom tree that is more than 150 years old. In spring, its petals flutter down like snow, draping the grass with light-pink impermanence.

Mum became a member when she was in her twenties. She was one of the first gaijin, first Westerners, to do so: she wandered in one day and decided she wanted to be part of this place that felt like part library, part guest house, part university campus. After a lot of back and forth, and being told that the right form couldn't be found and the right person to talk to couldn't be found either, she muscled her way in. With her membership and my membership combined, this place has been our second home for around 60 years.

Mum took me and my sister there a lot when we were very small. It was never a hotel to me; it was always our place. We ran down the corridors and played in the lifts and weaved our way along hidden paths in the garden, jumping over little bridges and rocks and finding secret places to hide. When I went back as an adult, the garden and its paths were always my first stop. They still are. Those paths have never lost their magic.

I adored the breakfast buffet. There was toast and cereal and fruit on one table; on the other, rice and miso soup and small tubs of natto, fermented soybeans. I would go back for seconds and grab handfuls of seaweed strips to scoop my rice up in. Some mornings there was folded egg and other times small pieces of fish marinated in soy and rice wine. You might be imagining a fancy spread, but it really was just like being at home: a rice cooker so you could help yourself, enough food to go around but nothing to excess.

The staff were like family, especially Ashiba-san. He was often on the front desk, and he let us come behind the desk with him, use his stamp on blank notepads and help guests with their keys. He seemed old then, but when I visited 20 years later, I found him still working there. And another 20 years after that, I found him again. That last time, he was in his seventies and had cut down his hours but he was still the same. Smiley, kind and dressed in his dark grey suit. That place was his home, too.

From this haven, we would go to visit my grandparents, my dad's mother and father. We were a single-parent family now, Mum and two girls, but Mum kept in contact with my grandparents and loved them. I remember very little from those times but have pieced together scenes from photos and stories and random memories. There were other memories, too, that I had forgotten about. Decades later, when I went to try to find my grandparents' house, to find where I had been as a child, I knew I was in the right place because my body remembered.

My grandmother, my obaasan, was called Tsue. I found out her real name only after Dad died. I was going through one of his photo albums – one of the few things that survived his death – and I found a photo of her. Sitting, as she always did, at the low table in that family home, her hair short, her eyes sparkly, her smile patient and warm. On the back of that photo, Dad had written her name. Tsue. I wonder who he wrote it for. Maybe for me or for my sister to find later?

Obaasan was kind and gentle. She would give us warm tea and rice crackers, senbei, and we would sit with her at the table, our legs curled underneath and covered by a warm thick blanket. These tables, kotatsu, are common in Japan. The blanket is tucked under the tabletop, draping over the frame and a heater. Another blanket goes over your legs, trapping the air underneath while keeping you warm.

We would stay cosy in there while obaasan went to the kitchen and back, making sure we had enough to eat. My grandfather, whose name I also found out from the back of a photo, was called Shio. But we called him ojiisan. He barely said a word, he would just sit at the table and smoke. I know he must have liked me because in one photo of the two of us, when I look about three, he is handing me a present, a toy car in a cardboard box. I'm wearing a red dress and we're both smiling. He looks proud.

Four decades later, when I decided I wanted to find that home, I asked Mum more about them. How did they feel about us, the only haafu, half Japanese, grandkids? How did they feel about us girls? My dad was one of three boys and his two brothers had sons. We were anomalies in every way. I wanted to know, did they like us?

'They adored you,' she told me. And then she pulled out a letter I hadn't seen before. It was written to me, just after I was born, and would have been posted from their home, perhaps written at that table. On one side was a note from my ojiisan, in the most beautiful Japanese script. Elegant and thoughtful. On the other, a note from my obaasan, her writing more childlike.

Dear Kumi, it said. Kumi, in the characters my parents had chosen for me. Kumi in Japanese, Kumi written by grandparents who loved me but hadn't met me yet. The letter went on to say how happy they were that I was born and how excited they were that there was another little girl, and they welcomed me into the family.

Looking at their writing, hearing their words in my head, I started to cry. That letter said something to me which, until that moment, I hadn't realised I'd needed to hear: that I was known, in a language and a culture I had for so long wanted to erase or hide away. That I was welcomed and validated and celebrated. That I had people who were proud to know me. That part of me belonged here. And there it was, indisputable, written in Japanese.

I had felt this ache before, and I would feel it again.

I would feel it every time I left Japan after a holiday. I would start to feel sad on that final day, and when I was at the airport, ready to leave, the sadness would rise in my throat and as the plane took off I would hold back tears. I felt the same as a child, when I left my dad after visiting him for those few weeks a year, even when I couldn't wait to leave. I would sit on the bus and watch him from the window, waving and saying goodbye, and I would feel my throat tighten and my heart ache and I would think back to all the moments I thought were annoying and regret not making more of them. A guilt, from a young age, that I had not done enough. Then I would think of him going home alone and feel sad for him, too.

Granny

Everyone called my Australian granny, Granny. 'How is Granny?' they would ask, as if she was the only granny that existed. She was always a Granny to me, her hair always white and pulled into a low bun.

The first house I remember her living in was big and two-storeyed. We would drive down what felt like a long driveway and park in front of her door. It felt grand and exciting. In her garden she had a chestnut tree, and a few avocado trees too. We would slide down the staircase inside her house in cardboard boxes, squealing with laughter as we careered down the steps, before racing back up with our disintegrating boxes to do it all again.

Granny gardened and baked, and Sunday roast lunches were a special occasion: pork and crackling, potatoes and gravy, beans, and bread with butter. Her table was laid with special cutlery – the smaller knives and forks on the outside, and the dessert spoon placed at the top of the plate. We learned to set the table at a young age and I loved doing it, making sure everything was neat and in the right place. I also loved putting napkin rings around the linen squares; my sister and I had our own silver ones, each with our name engraved on it. They lived in the top drawer of Granny's wooden side table.

Granny had a *traymerbeel*. I loved saying the word and knew it from a young age, even though I wasn't sure what it meant. I just knew it was the special name for a trolley Granny used to move food from the kitchen to the dining room. A few times I was in charge of it, and it felt like the most important job in the world. I took my time, making sure the wheels didn't get caught up on the edges of the hallway carpet, watching as the glasses and plates rattled on top. Later, when recounting stories about Granny and her traymerbeel, friends would look at me strangely. Her what? To me, it was like saying kettle or stove. Didn't everyone know what a traymerbeel was? I realise now that what she had was a Tray Mobile.

The house that meant the most to me, though, was the one she moved into after my grandfather died. She built a home near us, in the country, and it became a haven for me. She planted roses in the perfect spot at the edge of her garden. She placed seedlings in little pots on a wooden table at the back door, waiting to grow big enough to be planted in the right bed at the right time. Her cumquat tree sat at the front door, from which she would make jam every now and then. Inside I remember her bookshelves, rows of books about plants and animals, her leatherbound Shakespeare set, and her radio nearby. In the kitchen her pantry was always stocked with flour, sugar, dark chocolate and powdered milk, ready for baking.

Her sewing basket was often set up in the end room where the afternoon sun came in, and I remember on her bedroom dresser she had a little plate of bobby pins she used to pin up her white bun. And she had us, her grandchildren. And she had a sliding door that opened onto a patch of lawn. It was rarely locked. I could just walk in and say, 'Hi Granny,' and she would be there, somewhere, always. Always ready to stop everything and make me a cup of tea and a snack. My favourite was when she would fry up bacon in a pan, take the bacon out and into the bacon fat she would put a banana, cut in half lengthways. She'd fry the banana in the bacon fat until it caramelised, going warm and soft, and then she would pop the banana on a piece of toast and put the bacon on top. I would sit at her kitchen bench and eat it while she watched on.

It was at her dining room table that I studied for my Year 12 exams, my colour-coded manila folders laid out in piles. Green for Geography, Purple for Ancient History, Blue for Maths, Yellow for English. I would sit there in peace, hour after hour, rewriting notes and making flash cards. Every now and then, I would hear the sliding door open – the one that separated the dining room and the kitchen – and Granny would quietly place a cup of tea next to me. No words, just tea. Most often, there would be a biscuit on the saucer, a shortbread. She never asked how I was going with my study, never asked what I had learned or how I was feeling about my up-coming exams – and not for wanting to know. I always got the sense that, in her home and in her presence, I was enough.

At night, we would have dinner together and watch the news, and then she would insist that we watch something funny together.

She had a wonderful sense of humour: wicked, smart, naughty. Her favourite Aussie comedians were Roy and HG. *Kum, darling, we must watch.* And they would have her laughing so hard that she would have to pull out a handkerchief from her pocket and wipe tears from her eyes.

Then, other times, we would talk about words. I would pore over books she had on language and grammar, and read through her variety of English dictionaries. One set was so big, there was a separate volume for each letter of the alphabet. We would chat for hours about how a colon or semi-colon, popped in just the right place, could change the whole meaning of a sentence. Or how a dash could imbue a series of words with humour.

After high school, I would call her from my university college, using a pay phone. I missed our chats. One such time, she was excited because the Macquarie Dictionary had released its new edition, and new words had been added – ones that were deemed dictionary-worthy. *Kum darling, I note that the word 'fuck' has been added.* And she proceeded to tell me what an interesting word it was, and how, if the ending of it was changed, it could be 'so versatile'. *Fucked, fucker, fucking. True, Granny*, I replied and we continued on, placing many versions of 'fuck' in various sentences, laughing harder every time we thought of a new way to use it. This time, tears were rolling down my face.

When I was in my early thirties, long after she had died, I wondered what I needed to do to be like her. How could I become a Granny? I was pretty sure I wouldn't become one overnight. I felt like it was a series of decisions, embedded many years before I would reach granny age. I decided that I wanted a home where everyone felt welcome. I wanted to have a space that was peaceful, where people could be themselves. I wanted love to be shown through actions, gentle actions. Humility and care and curiosity. Letting my hair go grey. Always being open to new ways of thinking. And, a cognisance that, like her seedlings and rose beds, life had its seasons.

Connections

My dad was a small boy during World War II, living with his family in Tokyo. With Japan under attack, the government advised that children in Years 4 to 6 at school should leave the city and move to rural areas for what would be the final two years of the war, so that at least they would survive if the bombings got worse. Some kids went to stay with family. Dad didn't have family outside Tokyo, so he and some of his classmates were sent to the mountains outside the city. They slept in churches and halls and abandoned buildings, supervised by ex-teachers and other adults. Dad never really talked about this time but he did tell me once that when he first arrived, a nun handed him a sheet of paper with drawings of plants on it, showing which ones were safe to eat. The schoolboys were now foragers.

In that two years, Dad's mum, my obaasan, was able to visit him only once. I wish I had known all this earlier. By the time I was told this story, she was dead. I would have asked her – or had someone ask her because I didn't speak enough Japanese – what that visit was like. How did she get there? Did she take him food? What did they talk about? Did she see where he slept? What was it like when she left him to go back home?

Dad's best friend was with him in those mountains and each day they had to practise drills. Enemy bombers often flew overhead on their way to Tokyo, so the kids were taught how to stay together and get to safety if they got bombed. They would stand behind each other in a line, their left hand resting on the left shoulder of the boy in front of them. From there, they would walk together as one.

Dad told me once about the time there were bombers flying overhead and the boys lined up as they had been taught. Dad's best friend was behind him, his left hand resting on Dad's left shoulder. They started to walk to safety. A bomb fell nearby and exploded. Dad said he felt his friend's hand slipping off his shoulder and it was then that he knew his friend was dead – he'd been hit by shrapnel.

Many years later, and years after the Horsehead Nebula opened the door again for me, I was working on and off in Melbourne. I would visit him on those trips, usually only once, for lunch. Even though I'd felt our moment of Horsehead Nebula synergy at least a decade earlier, this still seemed like an obligation. But I always felt better afterwards (and, sometimes worse; as in, a bit sadder, a bit more reflective).

On one such visit to his little house in the retirement village, I knocked on the door and Dad opened it, welcoming me in his usual way. His eyes looked older, more clouded. Unusually, he was still in his dressing gown even though it was lunchtime.

He had lost track of time and was poring over a map of the Pacific, laid out on his round kitchen table. Various islands were circled and there were lines joining them to the United States and lines joining them to Japan. He told me he was trying to figure out where the bombers would have refuelled.

That same visit, he showed me some of his photo albums and pointed out a photo of another best friend, this time from high school. Dad is sitting on the concrete edge of a park. He has a winter jacket on, buttoned up high, and a scarf. His hair is long at the front and he is smiling. His left arm is slung over the shoulders of this best friend. The friend has short dark hair and dark eyes. He's wearing a winter jacket and scarf, too, and gloves. They are both looking directly into the camera, sunlight in their eyes so they are squinting a bit. They look happy and relaxed.

Dad told me that the photo was taken not long before they were due to leave high school. And that, on the day before graduation, this best friend was found hanging in his room. It took me a while to absorb what he said because he said it with such pragmatism, just another fact to throw into the mix. Of course, it wasn't that it was nothing to him, but maybe Dad had no other way to understand the sadness. I told him I was so sorry. He paused, looked up at me and asked, 'San Kumi, why?'

—

Throughout my childhood, and all the way through to early adulthood, I would grapple with what a good father was meant to be. At times, I'd make peace with mine but then I'd see so many examples out there, that would provide vast comparison to my own experience. In the movies, there were always scenes that affected me: dads teaching daughters how to drive a car. Dads hugging daughters when they break up with boy-friends. Dads leaving notes in daughters' lunchboxes. Dads picking flowers for daughters from the garden. Dads waiting outside parties to drive daughters home. Dads helping daughters paint new apartments. Dads being dads.

I even saw examples in real life. A friend was sharing anecdotes about her father during her wedding speech. One was meant to highlight his sweet ignorance about how long young women needed in a clothes shop, in order to choose what to buy. They were in a boutique in New York. She was laughing at his shock that he might need to wait a good hour or so, and it was a funny story. All I remember from it, though, was that she had a father who took her shopping. And bought her clothes. It might as well have been in a movie, the concept was so unreal to me.

But dads also shared jokes with their daughters and that is one area where I could relate. I should tell you about why Dad called me san Kumi, and why I hold onto it and how, now that I think about it, it really was the only in-joke we had that made him more than just a person, and me more than just a person. It meant that I was his daughter and he was my father and he had a nickname of sorts for me.

In Japanese, a person's name is often addressed with a suffix of -san or -chan. The older person, the one with more seniority and importance, is called -san. Children are often called -chan. So, Kumi chan would be how my mum or dad or obaasan or ojiisan would normally address me. It's sweet, really, because even as an adult, an older person or friend or family member might call you -chan. For a moment, you're little again.

For some reason, Dad thought it was funny to switch it around and call me san Kumi – a double joke. Such a small thing, but it means something to me, because there's a magic in shared jokes. They bind friends and partners and families, a unique glue that can't be transferred to others. That joke says, to me, that I had a relationship with my dad. And that he *was* a father.

So, while the other kids/women/my friends/movie children had the driving lessons and clothes shopping expeditions, all I had was san Kumi, two card games that he taught us to play, his harmonica which he would perform funny recitals on and make us laugh, and hallway putt-putt golf, where we would try to get the ball into the container. Oh, and we had one song. He made it up and he used to sing it to us when we were falling asleep on his pull-out sofa bed. It was called 'Good Girl' (though he said it in his Japanese accent), and he would sing it first to my sister and then to me, stroking my forehead as he sang it. Sometimes I sing it now, just in my head. I have never sung it to anyone else and I probably never will. And I think, how strange it is that there is a song in this world that only three people will ever know.

—

It was when I lived in that farmhouse in those formative years from late primary school to late high school, the one with the long verandah at the back and the cats and horses and ducks, that I started writing letters to friends. Postcards at first, from holidays to Tokyo (using a pen I bought from a stationery shop there, chosen from among hundreds of colours and textures) or the South Coast, where I lay on my back, still comforted by the blanket of stars above.

Time moved differently, I guess. Lives were lived in between school terms, and a postcard here or there filled in a few of the blanks. *Hi, how is everything? I am in (this place or that place). Then, insert what I have been doing. And hope you are having a good holiday, too. And see you soon.* At the beginning of a new school chapter, when we finally got back together in person, the real holiday stories were shared.

Over time, letter-writing took over from postcards as a way of not only connecting with my friends, but also trying to make sense of all my scattered thoughts and feelings. I loved sitting at my desk and shifting my brain into another realm, testing and teasing out my ideas without really having to go there. I could ponder notions of sadness and loneliness and fear, without ever saying: I am sad. Or lonely. Or scared. That was a step too far. It took me years to realise that although I felt I was being honest and open-minded, in fact letter-writing was another way to keep my feelings stored safely behind a wall of thoughts and ideas and philosophies, without ever having to be entirely truthful.

Example:

We had our Year 12 formal last week. It was pretty good! Everyone was dressed up and it made me think of how high school is over and whether I will miss it. I have loved certain parts of it – the friendships and community – and other parts, I am happy to see the back of. It feels like the right time to have a new chapter and I wonder what it will bring. Life is like that, though, right? There will be new chapters and I am sure we grow and change and that is what we are meant to do. Anyway, I hope all is well in your world and see you soon!

Reality:

We had our Year 12 formal last week and I hated it. I wore a red dress that I thought looked quite cool when I tried it on, but then didn't realise that black stockings looked stupid with it until it was too late, and when I saw the other girls' dresses they were so much more sophisticated than mine. I tied my hair back and didn't even have any make-up to use; they were all so dressed up and grown up and I felt naïve, like they had moved up some level in life and were more adult than me. I wonder if anyone else felt like that.

And then, there's the guy I took. Remember John? That guy I had a crush on for a few years. I was excited that he said yes. At one point, I couldn't find him in the crowd, so I went looking for him. He was outside, smoking with a few of the girls and a few guys, who were strangers to him. They stopped talking when they saw me. At first I thought he was just smoking a cigarette and then I realised it was a joint, and I felt naïve all over again. That I had never smoked weed. That I wasn't asked. That I was left on my own. I smiled and said something and then walked away, trying to be brave, but I just wanted to go home. Or, ideally, start the night all over again, but as a different person this time. I can't tell you how much I hate myself sometimes. I feel sad.

—

My friends tell me that when they see me in Japan, or around Japanese people, my body language changes. I become neater, more contained, more polite. I hold my hands differently, down by my sides, or in front of my body. I bow my head more. I don't realise but apparently it's quite noticeable – a form of restraint kicks in. I conform.

Or, to be more exact, there is something in the way that Japanese society behaves that suits me. There are rules. There are definite nos. Sometimes I find it easier, safer, to know the boundaries and the limitations. I know what is expected of me. And I quite like the rules. To me, they're about courtesy and respect:

Arrive early.

Bring gifts.

Take shoes off at the door.

Use two hands to pass over a business card.

Don't speak on the phone in public.

Don't eat in public.

That Japanese-ness suits me at times, a cultural protection. I like the discipline and I like the conventions. It keeps me and others in check and keeps things civilised. I remember one time when I returned from Japan, and felt the abrupt re-entry back into Australian life. We went from quiet streets and quiet voices and polite bows to a mother at the baggage carousel in a bright yellow T-shirt yelling at her son to stop kicking her ankles. It was all too loud. Too in-my-face. Not enough boundaries between their lives and mine.

—

For the past few years I have always taken a paperclip into the studio with me. I have folded it back and forth on itself, so it's about half its normal size. I hold the paperclip in my fingers and can easily hide it from view. When I feel like I am going to get teary or emotional, or when someone says something offensive but I am not allowed to react – because my job is to be neutral like Switzerland – I stab the sharp point of the paperclip into the palm of my hand. My body does the rest. It senses the pain, focusing on that instead of the emotions. Basically, I switch the emotions off.

I learned this technique from a former boss in a newsroom. I was about to record an episode on women who had become trapped in relationships and feared for their life. Their stories were harrowing and challenging. I knew it was going to be a difficult recording and I knew I had to be strong so the women who had experienced living hell, could be free to share however they wanted. I called him, even though it had been years since we had worked together, because he had helped me before.

That time I had tanked on-air, as they say. Basically, I had lost all focus in a live cross from outside a courthouse. I had jumbled my words, gotten facts mixed up, it was a disaster. And when it comes to reporting on a court case, getting facts wrong can severely affect the outcome. I felt sick when the nightmare ended, and I knew I was going to have to face reality when I got back to the office. In the 45-minute car ride back to headquarters, I prepared myself to lose my job.

I went straight to his office and owned it. I told him what I thought I had done wrong, and I shared what I felt like I had no control over – mainly, a lot of pressure coming from all parts of the network, which I felt incapable of warding off. He was firm and forgiving. You like cricket, right? He told me. Yes, I said, I love it. Well, when you go on air like that in future, you have to see yourself like a batsman out in the middle. You are alone, and your only job is to protect your wicket. Defend it. Don't listen to everyone else. Just do what you need to do and prevent any doubt from getting through.

It was some of the best advice I have ever received and I still use it to this day, closing my eyes before a big event or episode and imagining I am out there, alone, standing firm. So it made sense that I call the same person for hints on how to keep emotionally composed, in a room where others' trauma would be on display.

He told me how he had given the eulogy at his mother's funeral and wanted to do that justice by keeping his feelings as intact as possible. For that, he used a paperclip. It works, he said. But remember, you're supressing your emotions, so don't be surprised if they come out afterwards.

I found a paperclip, a green one. I reshaped it, twisting it back on itself to make it smaller, and I used it during that record. When a moment got too much, or when I felt like I was going to cry, I would stab the point into the palm of my hand. It worked. I could keep my emotions at bay and stay firm and present. I could do my job.

The green paperclip is still with me and has a special place on my desk, underneath my monitor. I still use it now. I take it with me when I know it's going to be an emotionally taxing record. I can remain calm and composed and let everyone else do what they need to do. I see it as a tool in my toolkit. On the days I don't think I need it but end up wishing I had brought it with me, I use the fingernail on the pinkie finger on my left hand. I keep that nail long, for emergencies.

But, as I was advised, the emotions need to come out, some-where, sometime. Outside my studio life or when things have built up over a little time, as a way of coping, I tend to go quiet, get tired, start to shut down. It's a bit like a hibernation. I'll want to watch something familiar – a favourite series, a favourite movie, something I've seen 20 times before. I find something deeply comforting in the knowing. Knowing what is going to happen, riding the tears and joy along the way with the knowledge that everything will work out in the end. Sometimes, I just need to know.

Every Living Thing

When my daughter was two, we left her favourite bunny in a taxi in Hong Kong. I think he was given to her by my brother-in-law's parents, sent across the seas, one of many presents she received. For some reason, she chose this fluffy rabbit from among so many other toys and he became her best friend.

We named him Fluffy Bunny. He became mangled and dirty and adored. To me, he was as alive as a breathing animal. He had a personality and he had wishes and desires, and he enjoyed certain things and disliked others. Friends had said: you must get a replacement, what if you lose him. And I said, yes, you're right. But sometimes, you know things and don't do things, and this was one of those.

When we left him in a taxi, we were heartbroken. My daughter was too young to really understand it but I understood it, and I wanted, more than anything, for him to come home. We made missing posters, his little fluffy face in the middle, his black eyes peering out. *Missing. Fluffy Bunny. Two years old. Much-loved friend. Last seen in taxi. Reward if found.*

Friends helped us put up the posters on light poles all around the city. They knew the importance of a little being, made of fluff and stuffing and seams.

We never found him. For years afterwards, I struggled to look at baby photos of my daughter because, in most of them, Fluffy Bunny was somewhere. On her lap or in the background or in her bed. In one photo, he is up a tree, propped high in a branch by a parent, but of course, she thought he was funny and did it all on his own. He made her laugh.

My daughter doesn't remember him, per se. As in, she doesn't have specific memories with him, just stories and photos. But she remembers him because when we talk about him, we both feel sad and there is an ache that we wish we could fill. And when I dig deeper, it's an ache that is not so much about us missing him. It's the deepest sadness that he is alone, out there somewhere, wondering where we went. And wondering whether he is still loved.

–

The Japanese/Japanese people/my people believe everything has an energy, a soul. Even items, even inanimate objects, like a rock or chair or a toy or a piece of clothing, have an energy, a soul – that everything is sacred. There is no delineation between human and animal and tree. The spirit world, the human world, the animal world, the inanimate world – all humming around together, all just as important as one another.

–

The last time I saw Piglet was when I was living in Hong Kong. I put him in a garbage bag with some jumpers and clothes and I moved house yet again, and then a year or so later I wondered where he was and looked for him but never found him.

Piglet. Missing. 15cm high. Dark blue with flowers on his tummy. Approx 30 years old but still a child. Last seen in a garbage bag. Reward if found.

—

I was browsing a tea shop in Kyoto with my daughter when my sister texted to say we needed to talk about Dad. She knew I was travelling and there was never anything urgent enough for a holiday phone call, so I knew something was wrong. My body knew it, too. I told her I would call her in 15 minutes, left my daughter with a friend and walked back to the little house where we were staying. I had a hunch this was a call I needed to make in private.

I opened the front door and walked up the narrow wooden stairs and into the bedroom, where the softest white light shone through the paper screens on the windows. When I called back, my sister told me that Dad had died, and I asked her how he died, and she said she didn't know. What she did know was that neighbours had called the police because they could smell something strange coming from his house.

It had been a relentless summer in Melbourne that year, with most days hitting at least 40 degrees Celsius. It was also the time of year when most people in Dad's residential park went away for the holidays, to see their family and be looked after by good daughters and good sons and good grandkids.

Like most years, Dad was alone, though I later found out that he had spent a few Christmases with the family of an elderly neighbour called Joyce. He helped Joyce with her groceries and would call her every night, letting the phone ring twice before hanging up, just to let her know he was there and she was safe and that she was thought of.

This summer, though, he was alone. And some time between Christmas and the week after New Year, he died. And because his neighbours were away and there were no groceries to unpack and no casual hellos to share, Dad's body lay still in his bed for a week, maybe two, and the days hit 40 degrees and the windows and doors were closed and when the police eventually went into his home, Dad's body wasn't his body anymore.

My sister told me this and how the smell was terrible and how the house had to be sealed off and how a Hazmat cleaner had to be brought in and because his house was so damaged from his rotting body, pretty much everything had to be thrown out. A health hazard, we were told.

I thought of his dressing gown that used to lie on his bed, the one that he would greet me in when he opened the door. I thought of his white singlets and how he would hand wash them in the laundry sink, resisting wasting money on a washing machine. I thought of the leather belt that he had to tighten even further the older he got. He had to make new holes when his waist got too thin (and then I thought of Alexei too), and I thought of how he would joke about having to buy jeans in the boys' section because he was shrinking.

On the phone with my sister, I could see everything in his small house. Japanese journals on the bookshelves, a years-old photo of his three grandkids taken the one and only time they were all together with him. A work photo of me that I sent him. I would have written a short note with *Hi, how are you?* and *Hey, here is a photo!* But what I really wanted was for him to be proud of me.

And I could picture his harmonica and his fax machine that he so desperately wanted to fix even though no-one used fax machines anymore. And I could see his quiver of arrows and his long bow in the corner of the living room, the same set I had seen in a black-and-white photo of Dad at 17, bare-chested, his bow raised high, looking like an ancient warrior.

And I could see a little pet rock. A small, rectangular-shaped grey rock, with plastic googly eyes stuck on it to give it a personality. I remember it from the first apartment, the one we used to visit, where we'd sleep on the fold-out couch. Where he would sing that song only the three of us knew and stroke my forehead. There, it rested in front of a row of books, and I would stand on my toes and look at the little rock and think of it like a friend.

In the ten years, though, when I didn't see him and thought it would be better if my life moved on without him, I never once thought about that rock. I forgot about it. But then, in that time after the Horsehead Nebula and before his body became not a body anymore, I saw the pet rock again. I would have been in my late thirties or early forties, and he was driving us to a local mall to buy us lunch.

As I got into the passenger seat, I saw it underneath the handbrake and my eyes welled up and my throat felt sore and tight. Dad must have moved the little guy from the bookshelf to the car at some point in the decades between. Now, its eyes were yellowed, baked in the heat of the car, and the black irises didn't move around anymore. But it was the same rock, stuck underneath the handbrake with Blu Tack.

It's the rock, I said to Dad. I remember that rock! Dad didn't say anything; I guess he never knew how much it meant to me (and I didn't realise until then, either); but when I looked at it and touched it, I remembered that I *had* had a childhood and it had been nice. And for some reason, Dad's pet rock now lived in his car, a permanent friend for his errands and golf trips and market veggie runs. I wish I knew where he had got it from. Was it a gift? Did he buy it for himself? Sometimes I think it must have been a gift but then, to care for it for so long, I wonder whether it was a gift he bought for himself.

When my sister told me that nearly everything was gone, I mentally scanned through all I could remember – the books and DVDs and archery set and golf clubs – and then I thought of the pet rock with the googly eyes and it was only then that I started to cry. What about the rock, I asked her. Do you know whether the rock is still there? What rock? she asked me.

You know, the rock that was on the bookshelf and was then in the car, I told her. I don't know, she said. That's all I want, I told her. All I want is the pet rock.

—

After the phone call with my sister, I left the house and walked back to where I had left my daughter with my friend. On the way there, on a main street that runs into the centre of Kyoto, I passed a small shop full of handmade ceramics – beautiful blue and white plates of all sizes. Little cups. Piles of treasures. I felt a deep sadness as I stood there, and it wasn't just about Dad's death. It was that I was in his original country, his place of birth. And how he had not been here, or seen this place, for decades. It felt wrong.

I caught my reflection in that window, the piles of ceramics merging with my body. And I felt a need to document the moment. So I took a photo: the face of a daughter, who no longer has a father.

Shaped by Moments

When we were younger, my sister and I loved movies. This was the age of VHS, and we would scour the TV guide each week and decide which movies to record. Once we had a movie on tape, we'd carefully place it in our collection, labelling the spine. We'd then write up movie descriptions on index cards, which we would keep in a wooden box. The cards would have the name of the movie on it, and they would be filed alphabetically.

Die Hard.

Outsiders, The.

St Elmo's Fire.

Top Gun.

Young Guns.

After the movie title, we'd write a small summary of the film. Maybe we put the actors on there, too, and the date of the movie. Those details I can't remember. What I can remember was the way we'd choose what to watch.

To decide on the one for that day or evening, we'd go through the index cards and pick out three each, and, through a process of elimination, settle on one. Round one: would we choose, say, my movie A over her movie A. Round two, the same. Round three, the same. Often, when faced with my choice over hers, I would actually like hers better. Or vice versa. So, at the end of the first pass, we'd have three movies left. And from there: which of these three? Then, it might be obvious (*Die Hard* versus *The Lost Boys*). Other times, we could get down to two, and then we'd decide to watch one first, then the next straight after.

It wasn't so much about competition. It was more about a diplomatic way to make choices, when both of us were so different in many ways, yet had a crossover of a love of movies and humour and, perhaps the most important thing, a shared history of growing up together.

Some weekends, when time moved slowly, we'd randomly decide to set up a mini trading day. She'd select things from her room that she was happy to get rid of: a stapler or pen or small toy, ruler or eraser. I would do the same, carefully going through my knick-knacks and filtering out must-keeps versus OK to give away.

Once we had our wares, we'd meet in one of our rooms, line up our goods and start the trading. I'd like that, I'd say, pointing at one of her treasures. OK, she'd say, I'll give it to you, if you swap it for that. Sometimes, one item of mine was worth two of hers, or vice versa.

At the end, we'd come away with new things – things we'd seen before but somehow they felt more special. I'd take mine into my room and arrange them on a shelf or in my stationery drawer, and put back the things that didn't get swapped, idly wondering what decided something's worth.

–

Dad joked that he never knew where to write to me because I moved around so much. San Kumi, he would say, are you living on a park bench? And even though I knew it was a joke and even though I laughed, there was a bit of truth to it, and I felt a hint of shame – that all my moving around somehow made me look unstable and that my life was always in flux.

Whenever I moved, I had a sense that maybe this time, I will get it right. This move, this city, this job, this person – and I will have nailed this life thing. Under it all, though, was a real sense that I just couldn't nail the brief. No-one else I knew – at least not that I could see – seemed so scattered, so unsure. I would dread catching up with friends I hadn't seen for a few years, knowing my stories would come across as a series of false starts and dead ends, while, invariably, their lives were progressing smoothly: same job, same partner, nothing to hide or be ashamed of.

By contrast, I had moved a lot and the majority of those moves were the result of me blowing up some part of my life and needing to start afresh. After a while, I got good at it, quickly packing and culling, deciding what needed to go and what should come with me, not holding on to too much. Knowing I could start over and buy a new bed and buy new shelves and stay up until midnight putting them together. So often, though, as I did, I would have that moment when I would ask myself: how did I end up here? Overnight one house became my old house and a new house became my home, and I would find a new café to become my local and new running paths to build into my routine, and I would find new ways to explain why, yet again, I was living somewhere different.

Sometimes, at night, I try to remember every house I have lived in and I always lose count after a couple of dozen. Other times, when I can't sleep, I close my eyes and try to remember my old commute in Hong Kong, when I lived in apartment four, or was it five, in that city. I can picture myself closing the door, on what I think was Floor 11, and walking to the first train station over a walkway. But I can never visualise the platform or even the train station, despite the fact it was my commute for a number of years of my life and I did it without thought. I knew which carriage to get on to allow a smooth changeover at the next station, from where it was about 30 minutes on a fast train when I would read my book or play a game on my phone. I knew that when the train curved around a particular bend and the high-rises gave way to greenery, I was close to my stop.

Those details I remember. So too the scaffolding on the buildings, made of bamboo and tied together by hand. I remember the night markets and the ferries and the trams that rumbled slowly across the island. I remember evening runs around the harbour, my lungs smarting with pollution, the smell of sulphur rising from the water. And I remember small bars that perched over dingy streets, where I would eat Nepalese dumplings and look across to air conditioners hanging on the sides of ageing buildings. Or evenings when I played my violin in a bar with random strangers who brought their instruments along too – the unassuming businessman with his roll of harmonicas, each in its own key; the electronic keyboard in the corner, beckoning anyone to jump on, usually after a few drinks.

What I remember most clearly is my job there. A newsroom in the New Territories, where I was in charge of a weekly social affairs program, commissioning stories, filming some, overseeing others. Writing and editing features to fill 30 minutes every Sunday. And reading the weather and sport and finance, and, eventually, the news (more on that later). I want to say, I found my tribe. But, really, I found a place where I could do the work I loved, work days that revolved around deadlines and teamwork and a sense of achievement. Learning about new things.

But I'm bothered that I can't remember the day-to-day, the things that actually make up a life. Where did I buy my contact lenses from? Where did I go to the doctor? How did I find all these apartments I moved into? I barely remember signing leases. I do remember a few supermarkets, but how did I pay for my groceries, was it card or cash? What about my bills and bank account and phone plan? All of that, gone. What have I forgotten that might be useful to remember? What do I remember that might be useful to forget?

—

For whatever reason, I remember a possum that used to visit us at our farmhouse. One night, one of us saw it at the back door. We cut up some slices of apple and put some honey on a few. I wanted to feed the possum by hand but when we opened the door, it ran away. We left the food outside and I waited a while to see if it would come back. It didn't, although the next morning the slices of apple were gone.

And so, over a few nights, we left apple slices outside. And every morning, they were gone. A few nights later, we heard a scratching sound on the screen door, and the possum was there, waiting. This time when we opened the door, it didn't run away. So, instead of putting the apple slices outside, I held one in my hand. Slowly, the possum edged towards me, me keeping ever so still. And then, finally, it was as close to me as it could get, and its tiny mouth and tiny teeth started nibbling away at the apple in my hand. I listened to the sweetest little *crunch crunch crunch* sounds, so loud considering how small the creature was. I could see its coat, clean and multicoloured, and the sharpness of its claws. The pink inside its ears. The light pink on the end of its nose. And the *crunch crunch crunch*. Never had an apple sounded so good.

The possum did this – or, rather, the possum and I did this – for a few more nights. It was always the same rhythm: post-dinner. Quiet. Scratch on the door. Apple slices ready to go. Open the door and crouch down, hold out my hand. *Crunch crunch crunch*. Then, leave a few more apple slices outside, shut the door and let the possum decide what next.

A few nights later, the same thing. But this time, I noticed something strange on the possum's back. A lump. At first, I thought it was sick or injured. But then, when I looked closer, I nearly gasped. It was a baby, the sweetest miniature possum, clinging onto its mother's back. Its eyes were the same dark and round, just smaller.

I held out apple slices to the mum, and she crunched and crunched. The baby watched. I could barely look at it, I didn't dare make any move to scare them away. I wanted the moment to last forever. The whole scene was so achingly sweet, I could – and still can – feel it in my chest. I didn't see them many more times, but the memory has stuck. It always gives me a feeling of gentleness and sweetness, and perhaps that's why they visited: to help dig beneath all the thinking and pondering and philosophising to an uncomplicated, trusting moment between two species.

Two Taguchis

In my first job in the media, I worked in an office where the journalists were of a standard above what I ever imagined I would be and I had a title which was Administrative Assistant. That meant I picked up the phone and picked up dry-cleaning and ordered cakes for birthdays and farewells and arranged couriers and, each morning, I would transcribe all the viewer calls from the answering machine.

I found this part challenging. The comments were most often critical: of the show, the story, the selection of guests, the host. Of how the show should be taken off air, or how it was a waste of money. I would transcribe every message word for word and quickly print off a few copies for those who needed to know, and try to get the copies onto desks before anyone came in. Somehow, I felt responsible – that being the deliverer of so much bad news made me responsible for ruining some-one's day.

The rest of the job I just loved. The office became my home and my colleagues became my family. I marvelled at how smart they were and how little I knew. I never counted the hours and I stayed back late and I wanted to know more, and in that office I felt free to be myself and they seemed to be OK with that.

One day, I went out for a lunch break and came back with a goldfish and a little tank and little pebbles for its tank and little plastic plants and a small container of fish flakes, and we all laughed at my lunchtime purchase and I decided to hold a Name Kumi's Goldfish competition.

I wrote up a sign for the fridge that held beers for us to drink as we watched our show go to air every night. The winner received nothing but the right to name my fish, and there were suggestions like Fish and Goldie and the then prime minister's first name (John) and the then prime minister's surname (Howard), but in the end I went with Buttercup because it was sweet and innocent. The colleague who came up with that name was one whose stories I always admired. He would find those human ones – the ones with heart and feeling – and interview people with care and write his scripts with nuance. It felt right that Buttercup came from that pedigree.

Every morning when I came to work, I would turn on the lights above my desk in the middle of the bustling office, and Buttercup would zip up and down the tank, so happy to see me. I loved him and he kept me company and watched the show when we watched the show. He was spoken to and included, and when I went on leave, someone else would change his water and feed him.

A year later when I left that job, my going-away present was a bigger tank, a square one, with more coloured rocks and bigger plants and a filter that threw bubbles onto the surface of the water. I set it up at home and Buttercup loved it and he grew even bigger with more space. He zipped up and down even faster with all the bubbles, and I knew he was happy and safe. Even though he never smiled.

—

One morning in this job, I needed to update some of my personal details in the HR system. To get into the database I had to type in my surname, so I typed in TAGUCHI and pressed enter, and was surprised to see two names come up.

Another Taguchi in the organisation, surely not?

And then I looked closer at the options, in upper case, for me to select:

A TAGUCHI

K TAGUCHI

Two Taguchis. The second was me. The first was my dad. He had retired but his name must have been left in the system. That's when I remembered: of course, he had been a journalist. A job offer in Melbourne for ABC Radio is what brought him and my mum back to Australia, a few years after they had met in Tokyo. And that one job was where he would work until he retired, broadcasting Australian news back to the Asia-Pacific, his voice familiar to so many listeners.

I had blanked out that side of my life, not even considering that my interests and my job were connected to his. But I had got myself a job in the media, at the same organisation my dad had worked for, and it was only when I saw our names together that I remembered.

He had even brought us home T-shirts once when we were younger with a kookaburra on the front wearing a set of headphones.

And as I sat there looking at my screen I remembered how he sometimes let us use his typewriter. I remembered the sound of the keys. I'd had only five years of my life with him before my parents separated, so my memories of him as a working father are non-existent. We had never talked sports or politics or culture and war, but perhaps there was something we shared that I had never considered: a desire to learn about the world and its people.

It should have been a moment of deep clarity perhaps but I quickly dismissed the coincidence. The fact I didn't talk about it with anyone else makes me realise now that perhaps I shifted it out of my mind because I didn't want to know. And there was shame in there, too: that my relationship with my dad was so slim that I had forgotten we shared the same profession.

Besides: I was still doing my thing independent of him, still deliberately distant, still a few years away from that road trip across Australia and the visit to his house and the Horsehead Nebula. But every now and then, when I let those barriers weaken slightly, I would think of that screen and our names there, together, listed one under the other, and I would get the smallest sense of what it felt like to know where I came from.

What We See Through a Lens

I once met James Nachtwey, one of my favourite photo-journalists, and wasn't surprised at how reserved he was. I had seen his photos of 9/11, capturing firefighters covered with dust carrying a baby out of the rubble, and a fallen church spire viewed through broken blocks of what had been a building. I had seen his photos of the famine in Somalia where he had witnessed people who were not yet dead but may as well have been: skeletons with flesh barely covering their bones and teeth protruding from drawn faces. I had seen his photos of the genocide in Rwanda. One stuck in my mind: a man whose face had been slashed by a machete, his scars so deep and wide they pulled his mouth back in a position that wasn't natural. And I had seen images of James himself, when a film crew followed him, recording him as he tracked maskless miners in Indonesia, their lungs burning as they carried sulphur through the mountains in wicker baskets.

I wasn't surprised at how reserved he was because surely there is only so much a person can see, only so much of the world's hurt a soul can take on, before words seem inadequate. For after each trip and each insight into gross inequity, and each insight into violence and revenge, there is a plane trip home and there are taxis and coffees and people complaining about the weather. And there are flutes of champagne at gallery openings and there are fashion shows and restaurant reviews. And I would wonder: how does a soul like his adapt back to this world, after living in those worlds, and how does his brain make sense of it all?

Sometimes, the brain doesn't. Example number two of a man who saw too much: Kevin Carter. When he was in his early thirties, he and his camera found themselves at the famine in Somalia and there, among hundreds of photos, he took one that ended up winning him a Pulitzer Prize – and ended up killing him.

In this photo, a little girl lies crouched on the ground. She is near death. Her arms are sticks, her elbows resting on the ground, trying to prop up her head. Her belly is distended. The vulture behind her knows that death is near, too. Even though it is in the background, it appears bigger than her and it is just waiting. Waiting.

The photo made that famine real for those outside the horror. But soon after it was published, the questions came: why did he take the photo in the first place? Why didn't he drop the camera and help the child? Pick her up and take her to safety?

His explanations were real – he was racing to the plane to get out of there, he saw the vulture only after he took the photo, he chased the vulture away, he could not have helped anyway because he was being supervised by rebel soldiers, that when he took the photo and so many others like it, all he could think of was his own daughter – but they were not enough.

And then the award came. He wrote to his parents and told them he couldn't wait to show them the trophy. He was signed to a prestigious photo agency. People wanted his autograph. But it wasn't enough. A few months later, he was found dead in his car. And on his note? *I am really, really sorry.*

And example number three. Another man, also in his early thirties, saw horrors that were not in existence until this day, 6 August 1945. His name was Yoshita Matsushige, a photo-journalist. He was in Hiroshima when the world seemed to end, an atomic bomb detonating above the city. Within hours of the blast that killed an estimated 140,000 people, he picked up his camera and his eyes saw singed hair and skin hanging off bodies like rags, and a row of people just sitting and staring.

All around them, the sky was burning and the buildings were burning and later he told how his eyes filled with tears as he looked through the viewfinder, and that what he was looking at was hell, and how all he could hear was people begging for water and how he saw a baby clinging to its mother's breast, the mother unable to move, and how another mother kept looking down at her own baby, imploring it to open its eyes.

Matsushige stood there for 20 minutes before he could press the shutter, he was nauseated himself and at one point, could not get anywhere because of the fires burning around him. But he knew, deep down, that surely this needed to be seen by others and not just him. So he raised his camera and pressed the shutter.

He did that four more times. But after that, when he raised the camera again, his finger couldn't do it anymore.

He lived for another 60 years. I have always wondered what those 60 years were like for him.

—

Anxiety would come in many forms. That sickness in the belly, my body wanting to escape something, an invisible threat that took over my nervous system. In my twenties, it was particularly bad. A sense that the walls of the world, the ones that seemed so open and transparent to others, closed in on me to the point I could not breathe.

It was paralysing. And frightening. One form of relief – temporary as it was – was to look through my camera. A Canon film camera back then. In that act of bringing a viewfinder to my eye – looking for something or someone to capture, and finding them in my lens – that tightness would ease. A literal reframing.

I loved seeing pictures and angles, preserving a moment on film. The way a building caught the light, the shadows in the late afternoon, the gait of an unnamed human going about their day. And waiting to have the film developed. I was told that, in a roll of say 36 photos, you would be lucky to have one or two come back that you really liked. I would usually like at least half of mine. 'You have a good eye,' people would say to me. And it was the one thing I could agree on, the one thing I felt like I was good at. I could see pictures before they knew they were meant to be taken.

I studied photographs closely, over and over. I still do. The framing: how one photographer places a subject right at the edge of frame, looking out beyond it, tempting the viewer to imagine what they are looking towards. Or how another might do the opposite, leaving empty space in front of a person's eyes, creating an entirely different story.

One photographer, who took images of horizons (to calm his brain after it had seen too much horror), had theories on how much horizon should be in a photo. Most of us, naturally, leave about a third. One-third sea or land, two-thirds sky. I liked to mess with that, and shift my framing, to give more of the sky. The result would be a bit uncomfortable, but beautiful.

At university, we studied imagery and were instructed that what we are told about a photo shapes what we see in it. The example we were given was an image of one woman's face, repeated nine times. Three rows of three. Her expression was ambiguous. She wasn't smiling, nor was she crying or angry. Her face just was, in profile, looking to the right.

Under the first photo, was a caption along the lines of: *This woman has just been told her child died.* Then under another, the same woman: *This woman is about to get married.* And another: *This woman has a few weeks to live.*

And gosh, how that woman's face changed, depending on what we were told about her. I could see her pain, the loss of her child. I could see her anticipation of a new married life. I could see her contemplating what was left of her days. I found it profound and jarring, how my opinion – and my feelings – could be so easily swayed, depending on what I was told.

–

I can recall three photos of me with my dad. In the first, I would be three or four. He is sitting on a sofa in what was our living room in Melbourne. He looks dapper: white pants, a striped short-sleeve shirt, a chunky brown belt with a sick brass buckle. His hair is long at the back. Tucked up next to him is me, wearing a sleeveless dress, pink and white. I am looking down and my left thumb is in my mouth, my left leg casually resting on his right thigh. His right hand is cradling my body. It looks big and safe against my small arm.

In the next, I am around 26 and slightly taller than him. Dad would be pushing 70 but looks much younger than that, and healthy – his eyes energetic. Our arms are behind each other, my right hand resting on his right shoulder, his left hand resting on my left shoulder. We look like mates, we look happy.

And the only other photo I can think of is about 15 years after that. Dad is in his early eighties. He is old. We are sitting at a coffee shop – him, cappuccino; me, maybe a latte in those days. I remember pulling out my phone – a sense that time was perhaps then, starting to slip away. I reversed the camera and he laughed when he saw both of us on the screen. It was the only selfie I ever took of us.

Understanding

Relationships

I worried, often, about whether the absence of a father would impact how I would be in relationships. It didn't worry me when I was younger, or a teenager – but, from my early twenties, it felt like others knew how to do them better than me. I would watch my friends, coupled up, and they seemed so much more at ease with men. They were still themselves and they could push back and say what was on their mind.

Me, I would not even know where to start. It was enough just to be liked and for someone to be interested in me. Their validation of me was more important than my validation of myself and I would, quite quickly, adapt to their lives and their ways of being. Their world seemed more interesting than mine – it was as if they offered some other place for me to go to and become. I would shapeshift and people please, though in the earlier relationships, I was not even aware that I was doing it. I would just slowly drift away from my own life and my own self.

It scared me and I had no idea how to fix it. I say that deliberately, fix it, because I felt broken somehow – that the deep fissure was, perhaps, irreparable.

(Show me a child at seven.)

And the problem with that belief was that the more I didn't get it 'right', the harder I tried. I had basically convinced myself I was starting from some subterranean relationship bog and I was blindly trying to claw my way to ground level.

I was good at working out anything cerebral that came up: living and travelling and sharing ideas about work; nutting out ideas and discussing whether to get a pet or what light fitting to buy. And, with each chat, I would feel a confidence and a sense of momentum: that I was building a united life. I was, and those investments were always genuine but, what got lost in the mix, was how I felt.

Enter Sara, again. After a break-up, I was workshopping how to tell someone close to me. I went through my thoughts with her: this happened, and then this, and our values were not really the same and maybe that is something I should have seen earlier, and all relationships end and that is OK.

Sara: You haven't said anything about how you feel. How do you feel?

My pause was long. I knew how I felt but my cerebral guard was so thick and welded on, it took me a good few minutes to even find the words that I might use.

Often there would be moments, internally, where my instinct would tell me something – that quiet inner knowing. But I would ignore the messages and think them away and, besides,

I was no good at this relationship stuff anyway, so who was I to know?

–

I am not going to go into details of specific people because there are two in a relationship and their stories are their own. But I will share a few moments that are important to me – reminders of where I ended up because of my highly honed, all-in-too-soon, shapeshifting, not speaking up skills.

In one relationship, where a house had been renovated and floor-to-ceiling bookshelves built and a courtyard set up for entertaining with a barbecue and the right wooden tables and chairs – the walls closed in and I felt caged – caged by my choices, trapped in a life I wasn't ever sure I wanted. I fought those walls for a year or more until I knew I couldn't stay there any longer.

The last month there, I knew it would be my last. Each morning, I would switch on the coffee machine that had been carefully chosen, and I would make my coffee, and I would stand in the kitchen that had been a source of joy, and I would watch the sunlight coming in the back window and make its shapes on the floor. One day, I took a photo of that sunlight, documenting it, knowing how much I would miss it.

I mourned that home as I was living in it. The sunlight, the jacaranda tree that sprinkled its yellow and white on the ground every spring, the pear tree in the front garden that bloomed to greet a new season then turned fiery red as autumn set in. And then, one evening, I put my suitcases in my car and said goodbye and opened the door to an apartment I had rented, and I placed the suitcases on the empty carpet and thought, here we go again.

Another relationship, I was looking after this person in a hotel. He was sick with an illness that destroys lives and relationships, but I stuck with it because we were a couple and I had hope. For the week or so he was there, I was racing between my home and work and his hotel room, making sure he was OK – taking food and everything he needed. There was no-one else to help.

One morning, I called his health insurer to see what they could do. He was too sick to do it himself. They said to me, he has to verify all this, we have sent a code to his phone, can you please get him to read it. And I said, he can't open his phone, he is so damn sick. They said, he has to. So I told him, please open your phone, you have to read out the code. But he couldn't, and I am telling the health insurer not to hang up because I had been on hold for an hour already. Finally he said, here's my password, you open the phone. So I did and I read out the code and then, underneath that, I saw another message.

This one, from his ex. The one who I had been told was crazy and he had cut off all contact with and yet there she was, on his phone. I opened the message. Regarding your current situation, she said. And then some crap about family and what does that really mean and what does that really look like and then – can you be a sperm donor?

You can't make this shit up. It was all too much. I yelled. I felt betrayed, yes, but more disgusted at myself – that I was looking after this person, cleaning up a hotel room, not sleeping, not eating, not seeing the signs. As I walked home, I thought: how the hell did I get myself here. How did I make this my life, and why did I think this was an OK way for me to live.

—

A counsellor asked me once, Why do you find it so hard to give things up? I was talking about wanting to toss something in and how that felt wrong. She asked me where she thought that came from, the not giving up thing. The violin, probably, I told her.

And I recalled how hard I had found it, to stop playing, to end my scholarship, to tell my mum, thanks but no thanks. For all the years of lessons and money and investment. After all that – and believe me, I calculated the cost in my head many times over – I could just turn around and say: I don't want to do this anymore.

It feels selfish, I told her. Surely, all things can be overcome. Isn't sticking with things good? Not always, she said.

—

Another counsellor said to me that I needed to look at how other people are in relationships, to guide me towards the ones I want. I had told her I was worried that I was always going to be like this. She told me I was going to be totally fine but, brain wiring, patterns. Look at couples you like, she advised me, see how they talk to each other, how they look at each other, what they say. Watch body language. Look to movies and books.

I realised I had already been doing this but had not prioritised the memories. I thought of a couple I used to work with, and a scene etched in my mind. They have a lot going on in their life and they have problems to solve. She is sitting down and he is crouched on the floor, to get closer to her eye level. They take turns in speaking and their voices are low and soft. She has tears in her eyes. They look strained, but not with each other. They ooze maturity and understanding. I remember glancing over and wondering: how do I get to what they have? What does it take?

What kind of person would I need to be? I felt both deficient and inspired.

And I remembered my favourite TV couple. Even now, I will watch highlights of these two, to implant their nature in my neurons. Yes, they are fictional but the brain doesn't know the difference. And going by the comments left under fan-driven videos, I am not the only one who looks to their blueprint.

The show is *Friday Night Lights*. The husband is Coach Taylor and his wife is Tami. In summary:

They are friends.
They are in each other's corner.
They have hard conversations.
They agree.
They disagree.
They apologise.
They let things go.
They say how they feel.
They laugh.
They are playful.
They enjoy each other's company.
They want to keep touching each other.
They are a team.
They are honest.
They are grateful.

—

A conversation, one of those ones you have in the early days of getting to know someone. Or rather, ones I have now – now that

I am older and now that I know where things can end up if these truths aren't shared. The honest ones about past relationships and what worked and what didn't. Disclosing what feels hard and sensitive, but necessary.

I tell this person what happened and where things went wrong and I say, It takes two, so it's on me, too – I chose these paths. True, he says, But I guess it is about confidence, knowing yourself. And I feel relieved, that perhaps this isn't about what was right or wrong – me being broken and flawed – just: I know myself more now, and I didn't back then.

The Ones who Survive

I saw a man trying to save his child and although I never saw his face up close, this person is wired in my brain.

I was anchoring live news, hours upon hours a day. Some days were slow news days, as we would say in the business, others busy, which generally meant something awful had happened to someone or some group of people or some country and, as a result, that story would become my life, minute after minute, sometimes for days on end.

For a period, the story that dominated was the Syrian refugee crisis. It began in 2011 and it is still ongoing. At the time of writing, more than 14 million people have had to flee their homes and have found new starts in Turkey and Lebanon and Jordan and Iraq and Egypt. The angle I was focusing on from the safety of an air-conditioned news studio in Sydney, was predominantly of the refugee camps. They were growing by the day and desperate, dusty humans would make their way to them, hoping to find safety – and ultimately, hoping to return home. One of the main ones was the Zaatari refugee camp in Jordan. If its growth was a time lapse and we watched sped-up footage taken over years, it would have been semi-comprehensible. Yet the inflow of humans was so quick and so huge, there was no time lapse needed.

Week after week, the footage flowing into the newsroom was mainly this, screen after screen of faceless, nameless humans crossing the border, and each shift I would try to think of another angle to their story – something to make their anonymity feel real. An aid agency, a humanitarian expert, anyone to help make sense of the geographic lottery: that insane luck that is bestowed on a select few, that where we are born, for the most part, dictates our life. Access to food and clean water and toilets and shelter and medicine, education and roads and hospitals. I knew, from early on, that I had won the jackpot just because of a randomness of my birth.

But, after a while, when reporting on a story day after day, one person becomes a group and the numbers become hard to contextualise. What's the difference between 20,000 refugees and 22,000 refugees? The extra 2,000 doesn't seem like a lot and you become used to the anonymous mass of humanity, and the images of hunger and thirst become normal, and you start to switch off emotionally. So then you try to find an expert to talk about compassion fatigue because you are fatigued and so is the audience, and quickly what was the main story just a few weeks earlier becomes a mention halfway through a news bulletin, parked between other world news and sport. And you realise that the images you first saw, the ones that drove you to seek that aid worker or hear that voice in a refugee camp, don't make you feel as much anymore.

They call it burnout, and there are signs. For me, I knew it was creeping in when I would walk out from the studio into the cool, clean air at the end of a shift and feel resentful of these other humans living a normal life, laughing and eating dinner, chatting about sport and complaining about the traffic. I would want to shake them by the shoulders and say, 'Hang on, what about *these* people, you know, the ones without food and water and shelter? Do you care about them? What is *wrong* with you?'

That was how burnout felt for me. A cynicism, a sense that the world is not safe. That it is unfair. Unjust. And it makes you feel separate. I would cross a line between being a participant in life, to being an observer of pain and, to cope, I would go home and eat some food and go for a run and unknowingly accept that, for a while at least, I would feel apart from everyone else.

And it's then, when my defences are down, that an image might slip through into my overloaded brain and decide to stay there, forever. This time, it was a father – although to be honest, I don't know whether he was a father, that's just an assumption that helped my numb mind frame what I was seeing and focus on one person out of the throng and shape them into a story I could tell others. *Do you care?*

The context is this: I am sitting at my desk in the newsroom, and I am writing a script and simultaneously glancing at the dozens of monitors bringing the world into my view. On one, the images from the live camera that has been set up on the border of the country that is seeing thousands cross over it every day. The shot is framed wide, and the camera is locked in one position. The humans are small and their faces unclear. In the time I watch, I can see at least a dozen people walking across the desert, and for some reason, my eyes lock on just one.

I can see that he has a beard, and by the way he is walking, I can tell he is tired. His head is drooped and his walk slow, methodical, not quite defeated but beyond exhausted. As he gets closer to the camera (I do a quick glance at the series of clocks at the end of the newsroom and realise it is early morning there and my brain can't quite compute that I am sitting in front of a computer and this man is walking across a desert and these things are happening at the same time), I can see that he is dragging something behind him.

It is pulling his arms backwards, and that explains why his head is hanging down and forwards: he is using all his weight and the momentum of his body to pull whatever it is across the sand. I stop typing. I watch him get closer to the camera, squinting to see more clearly. Another minute passes and then I see what he is pulling.

It is a beautiful rug, woven in reds and oranges, with diamond shapes throughout and tassels on the sides – a rug that would have been in a kitchen or in a living room, a place for a family to sit and eat, the heart of a home. But now it is carrying a small child, maybe two or three years old. I can see the top of the child's head, curly dusty hair, but I can't see their face because it, too, is dropped down, chin resting on chest. The child is half asleep, exhausted too, still managing to stay semi-seated.

In my story, the child is a boy, the man is the boy's father and somewhere there is a wife and a mother and brothers and sisters.

And maybe they would have sat on that rug in a place that was once a home.

I watch the man and the child until they pass out of camera shot and I never see them again. But for days I wonder where they went and what happened to them and I think about what a father will do for a child and then, months after, that image of them pops into my mind and I wonder what I am meant to do with it and why is it still there.

—

I become scared of what I will see and what will stay in my brain without me having any say over it, and, not long after, I see something else I can never unsee.

This time it was a series of attacks in Paris on a Friday night. 13 November 2015. Evening there, morning in Sydney. The city was still on high alert in the wake of the Charlie Hebdo shootings, the January just past, where 12 people were murdered in their office at the hands of terrorists. But on this night, the city was in a celebration mode. It was mild for late autumn. A football friendly was being played at the Stade de France between France and Germany, President François Hollande attended; couples and friends were dining at restaurants and cafés closer to the centre of the city, many making the most of the warmer weather, sitting outside next to busy streets. And in a music venue, The Bataclan, 1500 humans were being entertained by American rock band, Eagles of Death Metal.

Then, within a handful of hours and at six locations around the city, suicide vests and guns ended the lives of 130 people. Hundreds more were injured. The bulk of deaths took place at the theatre. In that building, 90 humans were mown down by gunfire – random, who made it and who didn't. There were stories of screaming and panic and of young people trying to escape and bodies piled up high. For the next several days that was the only story we told.

I was on air for hours upon hours at a time, trying to make sense of the attacks for people watching at home. I went from one interview to the next, watching footage of bodies covered with sheets and people crying and hugging and other people setting up makeshift treatment centres outside cafés. In between the interviews, I scanned for anything else online that might help me, anything that I might have missed. I saw a thumbnail of a video, with a caption along the lines of: *People trying to escape out the back of the theatre.* My brain is wired for more information and more detail, so I clicked on it without thinking. The footage was taken at night-time on a phone so it wasn't very clear but I could see it had been filmed from an apartment, a few floors up from street level, showing an alleyway at the side of the theatre.

As I watched, I could see dozens of blurry humans trying to jump out of the first-floor window of the theatre. Some leaped straight onto the ground, others tried to slide down a water pipe. There was no audio, but I saw what panic looked like. It was hurried and unthinking, there was no order to how people ran. Just this way and that, pure adrenaline, pure survival. And then my eyes latched onto one person among the rest.

I saw a young man from the back, in jeans and a dark jumper, trying to run. But he was slower than the others, who were all racing past him. He kept falling over and then tried to get up again. My chest tightened, and I felt sick, watching a man doing anything to survive. I looked closer and saw he was limping and that one of his feet was broken; it contorted at a gut-wrenching angle every time he put weight on it.

Despite this, he kept trying to run, the side of his broken foot hitting the ground with every step. He limped away from the camera and turned the corner and I imagine – I hope – he found safety and someone was there to help him and he was taken to hospital and his foot was put in a cast and it healed and he was able to walk again.

I didn't want anyone else to see the video of the limping man on his broken foot so, from inside the studio, I emailed the newsroom. *Hey, there is a video doing the rounds online of people escaping out the back of the theatre. I have just watched it, and I regret it, and no matter how much you might be tempted to click on it, for your own sake, please don't. Because once you see this stuff you can't unsee it and it will stay with you forever.*

I continued to wonder how else this man had been damaged and whether he would ever feel the same. How would he now view the world and his place in it, and ever feel safe again?

Places in my Mind

When I was in my thirties, Dad called me one day to tell me that my uncle, his eldest brother, was dead.

I have no recollection of this uncle and don't even know his name, but I must have met him because he was the father of my cool cousin. My cool cousin was all grown up and had a car and worked for Mazda. On one visit when my sister and I were kids, he buckled us up in his new car, which had bucket seats and padded seatbelts, and zipped us around the tiny streets near our grandparents' home. I remember our laughter was a mix of elation and fear.

But I did not remember my uncle, so I had no emotional response when Dad told me he died. Knowing Dad, that wasn't why he was telling me anyway. Could he be upset himself? I told Dad I was sorry to hear it, and asked, 'How did he die? Are you OK?' and then Dad said, 'Your uncle isn't actually dead. But he is dead.'

Now I had no idea what was going on.

'I don't understand,' I told him. 'He's dead? Or not dead?'

Dad told me that my uncle had a gambling problem and had lost the family money. He told me that my cool cousin had put my uncle in the car and then drove him to the north of the country. At some point, my cousin opened the door and told his father to get out of the car and said: 'You are dead to the family.'

I guess my cousin drove home after that and would never see his father again and Dad would never see his brother again and my grandparents would never see their eldest son again, and that was just how it was.

Mum told me years later, when I still trying to process all of this, that it would have been a pragmatic discussion, that my uncle would have been involved, that the whole family would have decided this is what had to happen. 'Your uncle would have known,' she told me, 'and he would have accepted it.'

Often, I think back to this and admire my uncle's clarity – the fact that he didn't need to spend any of his life trying to explain, trying to apologise, trying to get his family to respect him again. This way, the rules of the family had been broken and no-one wasted time and energy in that torturous grey area of wishes and shoulds and ifs and buts.

I tried to picture the scene in my mind, my uncle being driven by his son to the north, to the cold mountains perhaps. What did they talk about? How long was the drive? I thought of an episode of *The Sopranos* where Adriana thinks she is being driven to hospital to see her boyfriend Christopher, but she is really being driven to her death because the Soprano family knows she's been ratting them out to the FBI. When the car takes a different turn off the highway, Adriana realises they're not going to the hospital. Her face changes in a second and she just knows.

And I think of a scene from the movie *25th Hour*, when the main character, Monty, played by Edward Norton, is going to prison and his dad is driving him there. His dad says, We can keep going west and find a nice little town, and Monty says, No, I am fine, and they will find me sooner or later.

You know how they find people, his dad says. They find them when they come home. And then his dad tells him of the life his son could live and the places he could see, and then we see Monty in a desert. And you see them both driving through fields of lavender and they arrive in a town where they sit in a bar and share a drink. When they finish their drinks, Monty's dad tells him not to write and that they will see each other again, and then he drives off.

And I wondered, maybe he *did* do it, maybe he really did break free. But underneath I knew, like Adriana knew, that there was only one way this story could end, and that is the way it was always meant to end and not the way we would like it to.

My uncle knew, too, that there was only ever going to be one end to his story. When he was told to get out of the car and that he was dead to the family, my knowledge of his story ends too. But I like to think he found a place to live, that he found some friends, that he lived some years without shame. And I like to think his parents were able to grieve the loss of their son, and that his son, my cool cousin, shared memories of his dad with his daughter. I like to imagine that my dad smiled when he thought of his brother. But that is what we make up when we want a story to end in a way that has a softness of heart that makes us think, *Perhaps that which seems bad can somehow end up good.*

—

Imagining other lives was a way I escaped my own. Like a lot of children, I fantasised that I was in fact adopted and my real parents were some famous Hollywood stars. No surprise that one of my favourite movies was *Annie* from 1982, about the unloved orphan who ended up in a mansion and wore wonderful dresses.

Those imaginings came and went and others replaced them, but the one that was – and is – consistent is an alternate life in which I live above a bakery in Paris and write books. Every morning, I wake up and make a pot of coffee and when it is brewed, I pour a cup and sit on the window ledge, my knees tucked up against my chest. Some days, I smoke a cigarette as I look out to the street below and people watch. The cigarette bit makes me laugh. I tried to take up smoking in my early twenties to look cool when I worked at a Triple J; I lasted about two days.

In my Parisian daydream I am wearing a white singlet and white cotton underwear and the sun is shining through the glass. It is quiet and I am quiet and time flows how it wants to. I don't check the time and don't need to and everything takes however long it takes. At some point I throw on a pair of jeans, stub out my cigarette, and wander down a rickety flight of stairs to the street below. In the bakery where they now know my name, I order a baguette and secretly imagine the young baker is there for me to flirt with, knowing he'll glance at my white singlet and smile, both of us knowing what the other is thinking and both knowing that's all it will be and both being quite happy with that.

Later in the day I grab my one coat from the hook by the door, pull on some sneakers, pick up my keys off the dresser (every time I pick them up, they remind me that yes, I am here, I have a door in Paris and that door has a lock and that lock has a key and I have that key and that key is mine for now and that truly is everything), and walk the streets for however long my heart takes me. I look in shop windows and listen to a language I barely understand. I am on the outside of it all, but I don't feel separate. When I take out my key and open my door and put the key back on the dresser and take off my sneakers and my coat, I tell myself, *I am home.*

—

In another alternate life, I am living in Greece, in an unnamed town where wooden fishing boats dot the shoreline. I run a coffee cart down by the water. I make only one type of coffee – black, in a small cup. Like in Paris, I am happy with quiet. I don't talk much and don't need to talk much, but I don't feel silent or lonely.

And then, the more out-there alternative life is where I live in the sky, among the stars. I am young, maybe eight or nine. I am wearing a green dress and my feet are bare. I float around the darkness, peacefully, no fear, a gentle smile on my face. It is so quiet up there and the stars are always lit.

—

Every now and then, I still think of my uncle and I wonder what life he would have lived. If he were still living, he'd be close to 90, but I think he must be dead. I try to picture what those final years would have been like. A town where he was forgiven, and where he forgave himself. A life where, perhaps, he had a different name and made friends and ate ramen at a local shop. There is something comforting in the imagining and, of all the versions I can conjure up in my mind, I might as well make this one true.

Folding Cranes

Sadako Sasaki was two when the atomic bomb was dropped on Hiroshima. She survived the initial blast but, ten years later, her blood became poisoned, and she fell ill with leukaemia and went into hospital. One version of the story goes that a friend told her if she folded a thousand paper cranes, she would become well again.

So she folded the cranes, out of scraps of paper and the metal wrappings of her tablets. Her friends came and visited and the pile of cranes grew; with every crane made, a sense of hope grew that Sadako was closer to life, but really, with every crane folded, she was closer to death.

In Mum's Japanese classes, towards the end of each year when energy levels were low and the long summer holidays were enticingly close, she would rent a bunch of films from a special library. She would draw the blinds in the classroom to block out the light and set up the film canister in the projector. My favourite was

Sadako and the Thousand Paper Cranes. The version we watched was made in 1991, though there have been other iterations since then.

The film made me ache in the same way *Storm Boy* movie did, the story of a lonely boy who rescues three pelicans when their mother is shot. He gets them well again, naming them Mr Proud, Mr Ponder and Mr Percival. Storm Boy eventually sets them free but one returns. And that pelican, Mr Percival, and Storm Boy play together and run on the sand and even though it is all happy, you know that underneath it is actually sad, coming to a climax when Mr Percival is shot by duck hunters and Storm Boy loses his best friend.

The story of Sadako created the same feeling in me. I was compelled to watch it, over and over. The turning point is not so much the progression of her illness, as she gets sicker and slower. No, the turning point is when the real-life beautiful white cranes, each with a red dot on its head, stop dancing in the snow outside her window and instead, a crow starts turning up and its blackness feels heavy. Even though she is folding cranes, she somehow understands that the crow knows more than she does.

She keeps folding and folding, but she eats less and then, ah, *that* scene. I would both dread it and want to see it every time. The camera shows Sadako's room in the hospital, and the white bed we have become so familiar with, next to the big window looking out on the garden – and her shape we have become so familiar with, the way she sits and folds her cranes on the table that she can pull across her lap. But this morning, after the crow has visited again, her bed is freshly made up with crisp sheets, and the paper cranes are gone and there is just the emptiness where a girl used to be but now is not.

—

When Dad was ten years old, living in the mountains outside of Tokyo, the ones where he learned to forage for his own food, the ones where he saw his mum only once and his best friend's left hand slipped from Dad's left shoulder, the war ended. Although the Japanese didn't really know whether it was over or not. They were just told that it had not gone the way they had hoped. For weeks, no-one knew what that really meant and wondered if it meant it was still going and wondered whether it meant the mountains were safe or unsafe.

The voice that told them the war had not gone the way they hoped was a voice no-one had heard before and no-one knew if it was even real. It was the voice of Emperor Hirohito who, until then, was deemed a god. For a human voice to come out of a radio and belong to an emperor was a moment never dreamed of. And Dad was there. He told me, just once, that he remembered hearing that voice himself.

—

My sister's birthday is an auspicious day in Japan – 15 August. That was the day, in 1945, that the emperor's voice came out of the radio.

—

After Dad died, I called his phone, hoping to hear his voice message: *Hi, this is Aki. Thank you for your call. Please leave a message after the signal.* I called his number, but instead of his voice-mail, a robot voice told me the number had been disconnected. I wanted it to be different. I wanted to hear his voice as a reminder to me, *You had a dad.* And maybe a little nod to him, *You are not forgotten.*

—

In Haruki Murakami's 1985 novel, *Hard-Boiled Wonderland and the End of the World*, one main character, a solitary male, ends up living in a world where beasts with golden hair roam the plains. On the surface this world seems the best version that a world can be. But a condition of entry is that he has to sever his shadow from his body. The Shadowkeeper chops it away, and the shadow is locked up in a separate part of the city. Sometimes the man sneaks to the shadowfields at night and his shadow says to him, We can escape, together.

But the longer the man is away from his shadow, the more his memory begins to fade, and soon he forgets the world he came from, and forgets he even had a shadow in the first place.

—

After the bomb was dropped on Hiroshima, the blast was so violent and so fierce, it left on the walls of buildings the shadows of people who used to exist.

In that same city, decades later, a museum was built on land that was once ash and fire. On a wall in that museum is a black and white photo of the real Sadako after she had died, not the film version I knew – *the* crane-folding girl. It is dated 26 October 1955. She lies in her coffin, which is enveloped in flowers; her hands are resting on her chest, her fingers intertwined. Laced between them are beads. Only her face is showing. On her left side, a small doll lies next to her cheek, its eyes open and looking up.

Next to this photo is another photo of Sadako taken just a few months earlier. She is wearing a white sleeveless dress and is standing up straight, her arms by her sides. She is unsmiling. Next to her, a taller girl in a kimono smiles slightly at the camera. The caption tells us they were roommates at the Hiroshima Red Cross Hospital and the two competed to fold a thousand paper cranes.

The numbers vary and the story changes but it's thought that Sadako folded around 600 cranes before she died and her friends then finished folding the rest. The one thousand cranes were buried with her.

—

The first overseas flights I ever took as a small child were to Japan and we always flew Japan Airlines. I loved the logo. A red crane on a white background. Its wings folded up around its body, forming a circle.

Later, as an adult, when sharing stories of travel with others, they would tell me how nostalgic they felt, when they saw the Qantas logo – Australia's national carrier. A white kangaroo on a red background.

I told them I felt the same. What I didn't tell them was that my ache was for a crane, not a kangaroo.

—

All around Hiroshima now there are cranes. They are in every shop, sometimes just one sitting on the cash register. In other places, they serve as chopstick rests. In an outdoor roof garden, you look up and thousands of folded cranes grace the ceiling. There are bunches of them on statues and shrines and outside municipal buildings. And there are thousands in the memorial park behind glass display cabinets, sent to the city that once housed nothing much other than ash and fire, but now holds a coloured crane made by a boy called Johnny in Wisconsin, and a girl named Sally in Edinburgh.

When the city was being rebuilt, the mayor at the time, Shinso Hamai, wanted to keep what was left of a government building – the only structure that remained standing after the blast – in full view: its gnarled facade and crushed dome, a visual reminder of what had been. Some wanted it to stay, others were fiercely opposed – why see the horror again. But he was adamant. If we don't see it, we won't remember, he told them.

So that ruined building stayed as it was, less than a kilometre from where the bomb lit the sky and turned day into the end of the world, and where all that remained of the around 80,000 people killed instantly were shadows, and all that remained of others were bodies with skin falling off, and human-like bodies walking slowly with blank eyes.

All that the survivors wanted was water, so they found their way to the seven rivers of the city. And in those rivers were more bodies and the water was black, but they drank what they could and poisoned themselves even further. And then decades later in Australia we read about it in history books and are reminded that the Japanese were the enemy and we killed them Japs in the war, and we wonder, Do they deserve our sympathy? And didn't they deserve it anyway? And then you go to that city and you see an old man from a country other than Japan walking around with his hands behind his back, and he looks at the gnarled dome and he looks at the mound of dirt where the ashes of the unclaimed bodies remain and he looks contemplative and sad, and you wonder whether he was an enemy of Japan and what scars he carries, and what he is trying to understand before his time on Earth is up.

Sometimes I think of the 150-year-old cherry blossom tree in the garden in Tokyo that I used to run around as a kid. And I wonder whether it holds memories and, if it does, what it could tell me about the nights its city was bombed.

—

On one of my visits to Dad, maybe ten years or so before he died, I looked at his bookshelf and scanned the dictionaries. Two large leather-bound ones, Japanese to English, English to Japanese; then four small books next to them. Spanish, French, Italian and German. I thought those four were strange.

Why do you have these dictionaries? I asked him.

Because we needed to know the language of our allies, he told me.

Oh, I said.

And then I told him: 'The allies I learned about in school were different to yours.'

And later, and when the anniversary of the bomb came up, I thought, *If I have half Anglo blood and half Japanese blood, then does that mean I am technically at war with myself?* And I wondered how much blood was Japanese and how much blood was not, and whether I was therefore allowed to feel sympathy for the people who became shadows on walls.

—

When I arrived in Moscow, before the accident, and before Alexei and Mel and before my friend Kim and I joined a party of people we didn't know and danced to music we didn't know, another friend picked me up from the airport and drove me to his apartment. He was a journalist there and told me all about blood-filled syringes and his car being stopped by police and how he was tracked and followed. I loved every story and thought I was in a spy movie.

As we headed out onto the highway towards the city, he pointed out a sculpture in the middle of a small patch of grass that was hard to get to, and told me that was where people came to get their wedding photos taken. It lay long on the ground and was made up of a series of intertwining, open triangles. From afar, it looked like a long barrier and came up to around waist height. We laughed at how ugly the sculpture was and commented what a strange place to come to in your wedding dress, and I thought nothing of it after that.

A few weeks later, when I was on my way back to the airport with Alexei and Mel, after the accident, my face stained with tears and my boots caked with mud from the field where they showed us how they rescued people from burning buildings, we drove past the same sculpture. I thought about how much had changed in such a short time.

'Do you know what that sculpture is?' they asked me.

'Ah, yes,' I told them, 'isn't that the one where people come out and get their wedding photos taken?'

Yes, they said.

Then Alexei elaborated: that's the exact place where we stopped the enemy from coming into our city. It is where we stood up and fought for our country. It is how we changed the course of the war.

I never knew that, I told them. I felt immediately guilty for laughing at strangers who got their wedding photos taken there, without knowing why they did. I wondered which country I would die for, which country I would fly a flag for. And do I have that in me?

Wearing Masks

Journalism requires you to be two things at once: firstly, you need to be inherently curious and open-minded; secondly, consistently unbiased and stoic. You need armour to do the job well. You need to ask and listen, yet remain closed to what you yourself may think or feel, at least externally. This is a good thing to harness for work. Outside of work, not so good.

The problem became this: through my work, I was meeting people who were not afraid to be vulnerable and real. Or they were afraid, but did it anyway. One person sticks in my mind, Allan Sparkes: a former policeman who is one of only a handful of Australians to win the country's highest medal for bravery in non-combat situations, the Cross of Valour. On 3 May 1996, he rescued 11-year-old Jai Waddell from drowning in a stormwater drain. Hearing the boy's screams, he headed into the dark, unforgiving water, almost trapping himself in there and realising he might die. He was battling against time, knowing the drain might fill again. He got the boy out safely but his battle thereafter was with the demons that followed him.

He spiralled – the 20 years of exposure to police work became too much. At one point, he thought relief might come at the end of his revolver. A colleague walked in just in time and saved his life. After that, Allan decided he wanted to speak about what he had learned: about being open, about asking for help, and teaching others so they wouldn't suffer the loneliness he did.

That is the man I met in the news studio one afternoon, when he came in for an interview. I was intrigued by his story and had asked if he would come in to talk. Allan was on air for around four minutes. We chatted about mental health and the work he was doing with young frontline workers – police officers and firefighters and paramedics – to ensure they had emotional skills in their arsenal, to draw on if they needed them in future. I was immediately struck by his unapologetic honesty.

Afterwards, I reached out to him to thank him. We kept in touch: a Christmas lunch at his home with his wife and daughters, a sail on a boat around the harbour, a hike in bushland. He had something, *they* had something I wanted. Even just a sprinkle of it. They adventured and laughed and listened to each other. They were honest and real. I remember that Christmas lunch so clearly. I sat politely and chatted and made conversation, but I felt like a fraud. That beneath my words was a truth I was not sharing: that the person they saw was not the person I was. I wanted to be real, like him.

And that would happen, over and over. I would find myself saying how much I enjoyed interviewing that person, *because they were so real, so honest, so vulnerable*, before realising that

162

I couldn't even consider being that real and honest and vulnerable myself. But once that seed was planted, once I realised what I was inspired by – not money or fame or achievements, but honesty – it became harder to keep that mask on.

The problem was, I had no idea how to even begin taking it off. I knew I wanted to. What I would learn is that it would be a slow process. Imagine a graph, where a line creeps up, ever so slowly, across time. And then, towards the end of the graph, that line rises sharply – a trajectory that cannot be stopped. That's how it would be for me.

–

I got in trouble once when I was in primary school. I had a sore throat and wasn't feeling great. I was with Mum and one of her friends came up to us and asked how I was. I have been a bit sick, I told her. My mum pulled me aside and got angry at me.

Never say that, she told me. When someone asks how you are, you say: I am well thank you, and how are you? No matter what, say this: I am well, thank you. And how are you?

–

I am on one of my many chats with Sara. I have met someone and I like him and that is bringing up all kinds of stuff. I am pre-armouring myself so I don't get hurt later on. Sara tells me that I need to be more open and authentic, to stop trying to present the best version of myself. I tell her that makes me feel vulnerable.

What is vulnerability to you? she asks me. What does it mean? I pause. I imagine myself telling this person about other parts of me, the hard bits and the shameful bits and the sad bits and the wrong decisions and the regrets. And I say to Sara, It means you're not perfect. And she says, Wow. We need to work on that.

—

I went through a phase as a kid when I collected papier mâché masks from Japan. I had a set of palm-sized ones, creatures from Japanese fairytales. There were quite a few monsters, red-faced ogres with bulbous eyes and big noses. Another one had swollen cheeks and its mouth sat on the side of its face.

The fairytales, like the western ones, were always frightening. I had two favourites: Momotarō the Peach Boy and Shitakiri the Tongue-Cut Sparrow, also known as Suzume.

In Momotarō, one day a huge peach was floating down a river where an old lady was washing her clothes. She took the peach home and when she opened it, a little boy came out of it. He told the old woman and her husband, who were not able to have children, that he had been sent from the gods to be with them. They called him Momotarō, momo meaning peach, and taro meaning first born.

I would gaze at the pencil illustration of him coming out of the peach and believe it to be true. I would read about how he got stronger and stronger and how he was able to cut trees and how he left home with some dumplings to fight oni, monsters, on an island. And with the help of animals along the way he defeated them and came home with treasure.

And then there was Suzume, the little sparrow. She was found one day in the woods by a kind elderly man. The sparrow was injured and asked for help, so the man took it home and fed it rice, but his mean and jealous wife didn't like him wasting food on the bird. He kept caring for it anyway and came to love the little bird. I came to love it as well and wanted it to be better and wanted to care for it, too.

One day the man went to the woods and left the sparrow at home. While he was out, the sparrow ate some food and the mean lady got angry, grabbed it and cut its tongue out. The sparrow flew away to a bamboo grove and in one version of the story, the old man goes to look for the sparrow and when he finds it, the sparrow is OK and back with its family. For the man's kindness, the sparrow offers him two baskets – one big and one small – and tells him to take one home.

The man says he can only carry the smaller one because he's not as strong as he used to be. He takes it home and when he looks inside, there is gold and silver and all sorts of jewels. And the mean wife tells him that he is stupid to have taken the smaller basket. 'Imagine what we could have done with the bigger basket and all the jewels,' she tells him.

So the old lady finds the sparrow in the woods and the sparrow is kind to her even though she cut out its tongue. The sparrow offers her two baskets and tells her to choose one, a small one or a big one. She takes the big one and carries it on her back all the way home, imagining all the wealth she will have. But when she opens the basket, monsters come out and kill her.

–

A friend told me once that when she was a girl, her mother threatened to drive over a cliff. Her mother was stressed and was saying it was all too hard. And my friend, a little girl in the back of the car, cried and begged her mother not to do it. She thought it must be her own fault, and she said she would be better and do better, and she told her mum she was sorry, even for things she didn't know if she needed to be sorry for, because she thought if she did, her mother wouldn't get stressed and wouldn't want to drive over a cliff.

Later my friend told me that when she was an adult, she realised every time something went wrong at work or in a relationship or in a friendship, she would think it was her fault. In fact, she wouldn't even think it was her fault; she felt that it was her fault, because her body went into survival mode where her chest would tighten, her heart rate would speed up and she would think about all the things that maybe she did wrong. And she would start panicking and apologising, even though she didn't need to, because that cliff felt so damn close.

In a relationship, when she had a fight with a partner, she would immediately regret it and think of all she could have said differently and maybe, if she had been better or more supportive, they might not even have had the fight in the first place – so it really was all her fault. She then panicked that he would leave her, so she would apologise, say she would make it all up to him, tell him she would do better next time and ask him to please forgive her because really, she was a good person and please don't forget it.

Another friend told me about her brother, who ridiculed everything she did and hated her successes and told her she was pathetic and weak, and she believed him and even though she did well at school and in sport and had good friends, he hated that so much, so she started to hide anything she was good at and grew scared of doing well at school and scared that her friends were not the right friends, because she learned that whenever she did well, he would know just how to bring her down to size.

It would usually happen on the weekends, she told me. It was most often near the chicken coop or by the shed, out of sight of her parents, away from the house. She used to try to antici-pate what it might be that would make him angry – if she held her tennis racquet wrongly; if she won a game; if she got upset because she lost a game; if she got an award; if she buttered her bread differently – but the anger was so haphazard, it was impos-sible to know when it might come. Sometimes she didn't even have to say anything or do anything, simply existing was enough.

Most times he would kick her, though if he had a hammer because he was fixing something, he would ask her to hold a nail in place, and he would hit her hand instead of the nail, and if she cried or took her hand away, he would hit her even more. The hitting or whatever it was would always turn into kicking. And always to the stomach. So hard that she couldn't breathe. But if she couldn't breathe or if she cried, then he would kick her even harder for being weak.

After a while, she realised that after a session, he was usually tired out, which meant the violence might not happen again for a week. So, to have a weekend free from fear, she would try to make him angry, maybe on a Friday afternoon or a Saturday morning, so she could get the beating over and done with and know the rest of the weekend was clear.

As an adult, she told me, she would get scared for no reason at all. Like the time she and a partner were putting some furniture together, and he told her that his screw needed to go in there and could she please pass the allen key, and she started panicking and apologising and crying. And he asked her why she was so upset about nothing. She tried to tell him, and he sort of understood but didn't really, so she felt weak and stupid and thought maybe he would not like her anymore because she was too damaged.

She told me that she learned to read faces and moods and anticipate danger, even when it wasn't there. And how she always tried to fix things that didn't need to be fixed and repair things before they became broken, and how she still says sorry for nothing much at all and will then spend the rest of the day being quiet and good, so as not to upset anyone.

And another friend told me that he knew when he was younger how his night would go by the sound of his father's handbrake when he pulled up in the driveway after work. If the car tyres crunched on the gravel quite fast, and the handbrake was pulled with an inkling of aggression and speed, he would know that his father had a bad day at work, and my friend would know to quickly retreat into his room and pretend he was studying before his father walked in the door.

And on the days the tyres on the gravel were gentle and the handbrake was not so firm, that friend would know that things would be OK and he would stay out of his room and enjoy dinner and have a chat and tell his father about all the good things he did that day, and avoid telling him about the bad things and his fears and the fact his best friend wasn't talking to him anymore and that he was feeling stressed about an assignment.

He didn't even realise he did it, but he just knew it made him feel safe, and later, he realised that in relationships, he never told his partners how he felt or what was worrying him. He just told them all the good things and hid all the bad things and after a while he didn't even know what was good or what was bad – but he knew that being happy and not having problems was the safest way to be in the world.

–

I read once that in places where violence occurs, evil settles. The Belanglo State Forest is near where I grew up. And in that forest, backpackers were murdered and raped, their bodies left barely concealed. At the time the perpetrator was arrested and his seven victims known, I had just gotten my driver's licence. Often, I would go past that forest, knowing what had happened there, because that was all anyone talked about. And as I drove near, my body would start to panic and my palms would sweat and I would clutch the steering wheel a little tighter, and I would look down the dirt roads and wonder which one he drove them down, to their deaths.

And later, when I read about it more, police and family and other people who went back to that place, to see where it happened and to mark the trees and the ground – they would say how, even years later, they would go into that area and know exactly where those people died because there was a feeling. They would say how quiet it was and how eerie it felt and how you could sense death. How even the birds knew. That was the thing they said was the worst. Not even the birds wanted to be there.

Damien

I met Damien when I became interested in the young men who came back from war, changed, and lost, and searching. At the time, I was training for half-marathons and marathons and was working late shifts and early shifts and had no sense of day or night. So, a 24-hour gym became my second home; I could run there at night and be safe – although, afterwards I would walk home a different way each time, without headphones on and with my keys stuck between my fingers just in case. Because, you know, *being a woman*. It was at the gym that I saw muscled men with tattoos, working out with a discipline and diligence that was different to others.

After a few visits, I had a hunch; I knew their type. So I asked them, 'Did you serve?' One man there said yes, he did. He didn't want to talk but he said he had a mate he had served with in Iraq who was really interesting and was doing interesting things – 'Saving rhinos in Africa' – and that's how I met Damien. He was younger than me, tattooed like the others, and he had an intensity and focus that was disarming – and magnetic.

I learned that Damien had his moment when he realised he hadn't come back the same person as when he left to serve. It wasn't when he was working as a naval clearance diver, or later as a special ops sniper. After the war, he went to Africa to escape the destruction of men's bodies and minds and souls. To see life differently. To see life.

But while he was there he came across a rhino, dead, with its horn missing. This animal was bloodied and tortured and pillaged and destroyed. It was in this moment that all the other moments Damien had lived through and tried to forget came back to him. Real and raw and frightening. And the image of that rhino became embedded in his brain.

That trauma, though, became the moment everything changed. This was it. Damien felt it all and knew that this should never be. So he decided that his life was going to be different. He went home and sold everything he owned and left the country he had been born in and served for, and he made his way back to those dusty lands. He sank all his money into a new kind of war – fighting the people who poach these beautiful, giant creatures, and using his military training to train others to fight them too. He created a new frontline, a shield for a species that just happened to be put on this earth with a horn. Which humans happened to decide was of value. Not the flesh or heart or the soul or the skin. No, just this one part. The rest could be left to rot and become part of the earth, their particles and cells and sadness and fear, seeping back into the dust where their feet used to walk.

No more, Damien said on that day his life changed. No more.

Starting to Become

When I think of the things I started to do to become braver, to unmask myself, what springs to mind is the marathon I ran in the centre of Australia, near Uluru, the huge red rock that has shaped story in Australia for tens of thousands of years. For the Anangu people, it's a living, breathing landscape.

One late July, a few hundred of us lined up on the red dirt at the start line, crisp winter air in our lungs, waiting for the racing gun. There was a sense of silent wondering as the reality of what lay ahead dawned on many: why am I doing this again? Why did I sign up? Were we silly to travel this far to pull on running shoes and pin on a racing bib?

Why do humans even line up to run 42 kilometres? For most of us, there are no prizes, no careers in this – it is just one of those things. For me, when I read that only one percent of people in the world run a marathon, I thought, *I want to be in that one percent. Even if it's just for once in my life.*

The idea came on the back of two half-marathons, spread a year apart. The first I ran with a friend, the second on my own. In the second, I pushed myself until my lungs almost burst, determined to shave off a few minutes from the previous half-marathon. I smashed it, and by 'it', I mean my own personal-best time. That's the thing about running, the only person you are there for is you.

Once I crossed that line and realised what I had done, I thought, *Well, it's only six kilometres back home, I may as well walk there and warm my muscles down and see how far my legs can take me.* So, 21 kilometres turned into 27 kilometres; from there, my brain realised it was only another 15 to a marathon and the seed was planted.

A few months after that, a friend at work told me she was thinking about running a marathon and I said, 'Wow, me too,' and we said, hey, why don't we run one together. Both being journalists, we decided within an hour that we might run only one marathon ever, so it may as well be a memorable one and look, there is one in the central desert we could do next year. So we signed up.

Six months later, we were on a plane to the centre of Australia. The night before the race, we ate with the other runners, who talked of splits and gels and home-made protein bars. I had a few gels and a banana. What other races do you do, they asked. Not many, I said. This is my first marathon and I just want to finish.

What other places are you auditioning for? No others, just this one.

The next morning, we took a bus to the start line. It was magical. Remote. As we lined up, I saw the make-shift trestle table with a handful of marathon medals lined up, waiting to be awarded in a matter of hours. I wanted one. I wanted to be able to do this. But I knew I was undertrained and had not run far enough, and I had barely tested my legs on sand.

God, that start was amazing. We set off, and I smiled at my friend, and she smiled back at me, and we said, we're doing this. We ran in a pack for a while, until the half-marathoners dropped back, and the marathoners pulled ahead, and then, the vastness and empty beauty swallowed me up and I was truly alone.

I quickly learned the sand wasn't just sand. There were dunes and with each uphill run, there was a downhill equivalent; that's when the sand would pile into my shoes and take up whatever room was left for my toes. At the bottom of each dune, I hurriedly took off a shoe and emptied it and then took off the other shoe and emptied it, trying to keep moving because if I stopped I knew I would never be able to start running again.

I ran past a row of lemon trees and, still on a high from the start of the race, marvelled at their ability to survive and thrive. Later, so much later, the thought of those lemons trees was the only thing that kept me going. *One more kilometre*, I would tell myself, *and maybe I will come across those trees.* I would imagine picking up a lemon and ripping it apart with my hands and sucking the tart juice from the flesh, and I thought, *This is a different level of being human.*

I had read books and articles and inspiration quotes of this mad race some of us humans do. You know the ones: *If you don't know yourself at the end of a marathon, you never will. Perseverance. Never give up.* One image stuck in my mind: a man, wearing layer upon layer of winter gear, running knee-deep in snow. He was training for a marathon. *If he can do it, so can I*, I thought.

But, at around 27 kilometres into my race, I wasn't sure I could. I had heard of 'the wall' and read about the wall, and I hit that wall. For me it came in the form of panic and tears – not so much physical exhaustion but the mental realisation that I had so much further to go. The joy had disappeared. I was in the middle of nowhere, literally, and I didn't think I had it in me to keep going.

That's when my mind started trying to make me give up. I thought of a man at the start line who had a small teddy bear strapped to his back. He was running for a kids' cancer charity and the bear was the mascot. *Ah, see, he needs to finish*, my brain told me, because he is raising money and he has people relying on him to cross that line – but me, there is no *real* reason for me to get through this.

And, at the 28-kilometre mark, my brain told me that I had run further than I had ever run before, so it wouldn't matter if I stopped now. In fact, I should be *proud* of myself and this would not be a failure. And just as I was thinking that, I saw another runner in front of me, maybe five minutes ahead, stop. He had come across one of the race crew trucks and I saw him stop and get inside and my brain told me that if even he had pulled out, when he was fitter and faster than me, then this race must be hard.

As I got closer to the man and the truck, I could see he was sipping an energy drink and looking oh-so relieved and I wanted to do the same. But. I also didn't. I didn't want to give up. And it wasn't so much that I didn't want to give up on the race. I didn't want to give up on myself, and that is the thing about running 42 kilometres: you want this for you. Not for a lover or a work-place or a child or a family or a friend. You want this for you.

I ran past the truck and the man inside sipping the sports drink. As I passed by, I put my head down, not wanting to see my last chance to escape. I rounded the next corner and, for the first time in such a long time, perhaps the first time ever, I backed myself.

I ran each excruciating kilometre after that, and I came across the lemon trees. As I ran, I picked a lemon off the ground, ripped into its skin, grasped the flesh out of the skin with my teeth, and thanked whoever had planted the trees and thanked nature for growing something that could thrive and sustain. That sugar and liquid got me through the next bit and the next bit after that.

With a few kilometres to go, I started to see other runners again. Strangers who had crossed the line minutes or hours before came back and ran with me in that last stretch. One man, jogging alongside me, said he was proud of me and told me I was nearly there. Another asked if this was my first marathon and when I replied yes, he said I should be proud. And then, my friend, who had skipped across the finish line at least half an hour before me, ran up to me, beaming. You're nearly there.

She ran with me to the finish line but let me cross on my own. We picked up our medals and we took photos of our dusty shoes in ancient red dirt and though I couldn't articulate it then, I knew deep down that when you do something like that, you don't really come back the same person.

–

Six months after I ran with my demons on the dry red earth, I was on a 70-foot yacht, sailing what's thought to be one of the hardest ocean races in the world – the Sydney to Hobart.

Six hundred and thirty nautical miles, taking however long it takes. I had nabbed a media spot on a boat with around 20 others. Despite a previous race when I was living in Hong Kong where I got seasick and vowed I'd never go on a boat again, I found myself taking on this challenge simply because an opportunity came up and I didn't want to miss it.

Who gets to do this, I told myself – it's a once-in-a-lifetime chance that you grab when you can. The desire comes first; the fear and the questioning come after. But by then, it's too late – you've already signed on and you're committed and maybe that's why we sign up and turn up.

For me, that race was five days on the open ocean, working four-hour shifts around the clock, cleaning and cooking and taking seasickness tablets every eight hours. Day was night and night was day and time became relevant only to the rhythms of our boat. We felt tiredness beyond tired and lived on top of each other – sharing one toilet, the 'heads', in its tiny, cramped space, with barely a curtain separating it from the rest of the crew. It wasn't uncommon to hear someone swearing because the toilet wouldn't 'flush' – a pump is meant to get rid of any waste – then emerge with their business in a plastic bag, having scooped it up, to then throw it overboard. Dignity took a back seat.

Getting dressed was crushingly difficult and took 30 minutes. We had to pull on layers of thermals and then overalls, trying to balance as the boat heeled left and right, trying not to dislocate a shoulder while lifting a foot to put it into a trouser leg. Everything, absolutely everything, was a battle – against the noise and the boat and the waves and the movement.

And then there was the loneliness. It was that worst kind, where you are surrounded by people but each is in their own world, and each is on that boat for their own soul-deep reasons, and each is tired beyond tired, and fighting their own bodies and their own ghosts. So you retreat into yourself, the only common goals being to stay safe and to reach the next port.

My bunk was called the letterbox, three levels up, so small that it was impossible to sit up in. Imagine slotting a letter into a letterbox. To access it, there was a narrow opening where I had to ninja climb up the wall and fling myself into it virtually horizontally. And then I had to try to sleep. It's difficult to describe the noise. Every few seconds, 30 tonnes of steel slammed into the power of the ocean, head-on. *Bang, bang, bang, bang.* I clung onto the side of the bunk, half asleep, knowing if I slept properly I might roll out onto the floor. So I half-dozed and listened to the yells on deck, knowing how cold it was out there and how relentless, and I was grateful it wasn't me – but in a few hours it would be.

When we were training a few weeks earlier, we did a man overboard drill with a life-sized dummy in calmer waters. We were sailing and the dummy was dropped into the sea; as trained, one of us spotted it and kept our finger pointed towards it. We dropped a marker in the ocean and turned the boat around, hoisting sails and tacking and yelling out instructions. It took us nearly ten minutes to fetch the dummy. What I learned then was that if any of us fell into the ocean, at night, with a southerly barrelling into us that continued for three days straight – well, we would never be found.

–

During the training, I met Juerg. He was an adventurer and a photographer, mainly focusing his lens on ocean races. I volunteered to go up the mast and I'm scared of heights, so he decided to come up with me.

When we were so far up I could not make out any person below me on the deck, Juerg told me to go out onto the spreaders – the parts of the mast that come out horizontally – so he could take some photos. It was terrifying. My legs started shaking and I felt sick: my body in total survival mode. I had a harness on so there was no way I could die, but it didn't feel that way. I was recording it all on a GoPro. When I watch that clip, even now, I can hear my fear, a groaning, as if I am trying to urge my body to do the opposite of what it wants. And then I can hear this interaction:

Juerg: You are OK, you are not going to fall.

Me: OK.

Juerg: You are not going to fall.

Me: OK.

Juerg: You can be scared or you can enjoy it.

Me: OK, I'm going to enjoy it.

I then urge the team below me, so far below me on that tiny deck, to hoist me up even higher to get me to the next spreader. You can hear the shift in my voice. I've made the decision that I am going to decide to enjoy this, so I may as well go all the way.

In the years after that, when I find I have fallen back to a smaller version of myself, I will look back at the photos Juerg took and I will imprint them in my brain. And I will remember his voice: *You can be scared or you can enjoy it.*

—

On one night shift during the race, I was below deck when a sail was pulled down and shoved down the hatch. The job then, for whoever happened to be below, was to 'wool' the sail. Basically, find its top, find its edges and corners, and stretch it down the length of the boat, past sleeping sailors, so it could be rolled up properly. It needed two people to do it, and it was just the luck, or unluck, of the draw as to who would have to do it.

Once the sail was rolled the right way, we would take lengths of wool, which one of us had already cut up – maybe this shift, maybe the last – and tie strand after strand around the sail, knotting each length twice. The knots had to be firm but not too firm, so that when the sail was hoisted again the wool pieces would just break apart, letting the sail unfurl and take on the wind.

I was beyond tired when that sail came down the hatch, and immediately rued my luck that I happened to be below deck. A colleague and I did the duty, finding the edges and the corners, rolling, wooling. It took us over an hour. That is the work, the hard work, the grunt. We finished and called up the hatch and heaved its weight above, so that it would rest on the side of the deck, waiting for the time when the wind would drop or gather speed and it would be hoisted again.

Job done, I thought. And just as we were heading up the stairs, I heard the same cry, the same sound of a sail being pulled off the mast, and down the hatch came another sail. Another one to be rolled up and wooled. The sail we had just finished was being hauled up the mast again.

'No,' I said, 'surely not. I can't do this again. I just can't.'

'You have to, we have to,' my fellow sailor said.

'But we just did one,' I told him. 'Can't someone else do it?'

'We have to,' he told me, 'we're here. It's the job.'

I wanted to stomp and slam a door and throw a tantrum. It all felt so unfair and this irrational part of me rose up and wanted to fight, or sit down and cry. Like a child not getting its way. But that's not how it works on a boat. 'OK,' I said, 'just give me a few minutes.' And I sat on the edge of a bunk and closed my eyes and felt sorry for myself, for the smallest moment. And I dragged myself up the ladder and let my face feel the cool, salty night air. I breathed it in, and I let a few tears go, and I went down the ladder and said to him, 'OK, let's do it, but let's get it done in 30 minutes. Let's smash this thing.' And we did.

Strange what we can do when we get out of our own way.

And there were rewards. Rewards for accepting what is, for accepting that the wind won't do what you want it to, for accepting that you might have to wool two sails when someone else hasn't done it for days. For accepting that you are living with little dignity but so is everyone else. For me, those rewards came in the form of nature.

I would look at the stars on a quiet night – when the boat was gliding, at one with its ocean path below – and I saw what other adventurers saw, I imagined them navigating their way to new lands with just animal skin for warmth. No emergency beacons or race trackers or GPS or Gore-Tex. Humans, across time, doing the same thing, seeing the same sky, feeling the same wind. And I would feel differently about my place in the universe. I would feel at once connected to history and, at the same time, wonderfully insignificant. What will be, will be.

There was the time about 2 am or 3 am when I was sitting on the deck, hunched over and pulling the hood of my jacket over my face as much as I could, and the waves around the edges of the boat glowed an unearthly green. Phosphorescence, so unreal it was as if it was manufactured in a laboratory, but here it was, surrounding our vessel, reassuring us with its glow.

And once in a daylight moment, a pod of dolphins raced alongside us, their snouts in the whitewash, the water gliding off their backs as if they were part of the ocean and the ocean was part of them. They stayed with us for a few minutes, guiding us through their home, as if to say, You're not alone. Look at us, we're safe here and so are you.

In another rare calm patch, when the ocean and the boat and the wind danced gently and we sat on the deck and had the chance to chat and find out a bit more about each other: there was the cordial maker who named a flavour 'Love' for his wife; a woman who sold all she owned after her 12-year marriage ended and decided to sail around the world; and the young helmsman, who didn't say much, but the way he skipped lightly on the deck made us all think he was more comfortable on the sea than he would have been on land. I spotted a turtle floating on its back in the vast ocean. *What are you doing here, little guy?* I whispered to him. *Where are you going?* But mainly, *thank you for being here.*

And one time our skipper pointed ahead to the blackest clouds on the horizon and said, 'That is where we are headed, right into that storm, that is our direction.' And I thought, *This is crazy, we should be heading away from that, we're going to die.* At that exact moment, a shaft of sunlight shone directly through the stormy black, right to the point we were aiming for, as if to say, It's OK. I've got your back.

—

They were the moments when I would think, Now I get it. Now I have found a new level of strength, of knowing. I can do this life thing better, thanks to this red dirt and the endless ocean. But then I would slip back, ever so gradually. Lose some of that power I had found in myself, lose some of the sense that I was creating my own story, and slip back into patterns, slip back into pleasing and being good and saying the right things at the right time and not causing waves and not saying, I've had enough.

The shifts would be so incremental, I wouldn't even realise I was somewhere else, and even if I did, I would not know where I had gone to. Sometimes I was so far away from myself, it would take the biggest, brightest neon sign saying, 'Turn Left HERE you dumbass, you have gone waaaayy off track' to get me back to where I needed to be.

Linda

'Hi, the Dump'. That's how messages between Linda and me start. 'Dump' for 'dumpling', because she has Chinese heritage and I have Japanese heritage, and the first meals we shared were plates of dumplings near our work. To me, Linda is not Linda, she is my Dumpy. And I am the same to her. We share a name.

I remember the day I decided to really speak to her, and by that I mean, to be honest. Until then, our interactions had been lovely and friendly: chats about our industry and our where-to-nexts. We had the same energy and zest for life. We loved to workshop ideas. We liked sharing hacks and tricks of how we could be more creative and productive. We both liked to grow and be challenged.

Later, I would realise, we had similar insecurities and 'tender spots', as we like to call them. That knowledge, intricate and honest, came a few years after we met, just as a long Covid lockdown phone call was about to end. I had been walking around my neighbourhood and we had spoken for close to an hour: how we were feeling about the lockdown (for her, it meant she was unable to join her partner overseas), how long we thought this would go for, what was going on with our respective work. Then, and I remember this so clearly – I was nearly home and I looked over at a verge of grass on the side of the road and for some reason, I had the strongest feeling that I needed to tell her more. Perhaps because we were isolated and life was so stripped back, I felt there was no reason for all the usual protections.

So, I sat down on the grass and I told her more of what was really going on in my life. Things I had not voiced to others. Things I had barely wanted to acknowledge myself. Things I was embarrassed about, scared about, fearful of.

I talked and she listened and at one point, we turned on our cameras and we chatted to each other's faces. I took a screenshot of that moment, knowing it was something special. A moment to mark and remember. And then she told me more about how she was really feeling and I listened, and from there, our friendship became real, and unusual. One that grew predominantly through voice messages.

On long walks, I would tell her how I was feeling, or about my day, or how I was going to tackle this problem or that. Somehow, in hearing my own voice articulate ideas and fears and dread, I was able to make more sense of them. And she would do the same. Talk, listen, respond. Talk, listen, respond. On any day, even now, we will share dozens of voice messages – sometimes about nothing – *Am picking up coffee* – other times, *Feeling flat today.*

And this is the thing. Sharing my days, often hour by hour – where I'm going, who I'm meeting up with, what dinner I'm cooking, what creative block I'm trying to solve – creates a picture intimate enough that there's nowhere to hide. It's a place for both of us to be vulnerable. And forgiving. Of ourselves. A place where shame has no time to accrue. A place where imperfection is understood. No performing. No pretending.

And on the days when one of us is up and the other is down, where one of us apologises for a download that might be full of anxiety and doubt, the other will always say: *You don't need to be sorry. Remember, we meet each other where we are at. That is what us Dumps do.*

And that is what we did, when I got a text from her, early one Saturday morning. *Dumpy, I have been in a car crash. I am OK.* And from there: knowing that her partner had left the night before to go back overseas, I told her I would come to the hospital, and she said, 'Yes please', instead of 'Don't worry.' Then I picked up nice food for her on the way and tried not to drive too fast, even though I wanted to be there in a second. I parked the car in a big hospital car park and found my way to her ward, walked past the nurse's station, found her room and saw her in the bed, not in her own clothes but in a gown.

Both of us cried when we saw each other. 'Thank you for letting me come to be with you,' I told her. 'Thank you for being here,' she said back. And then I asked, 'How is your baby?' Linda was six months pregnant. 'I think she is OK. I can still feel her,' she told me.

And we cried some more and I gave her some of my comfy clothes to wear so she could feel half normal, ones I had thrown into a bag as I rushed out the door. And we waited for checks and we went to get an MRI and an ultrasound, and when I sat there next to her and we saw the image of her unborn baby moving around, and we heard her heartbeat, I pulled out my phone and recorded the sound of her daughter. Safe in the womb. Knowing that had Linda been driving one second faster or one second slower, the drunk driver that ploughed into the side of her car could have killed them both.

Business Cards

My boss in my newsroom in Hong Kong asked me whether I would like to try reading the weather. I was in my early thirties and in charge of a weekly social affairs program, finding those stories that were sometimes tender and sometimes tough.

I delved into smoking bans and breastfeeding and young girls who pretended they were going overseas to study, but really they had fallen pregnant and were living in a building in their home city, only to emerge seven or eight months later, looking the same except they had had a baby and that baby had been given away and now their lives could return to normal.

I filmed in shopping malls with suicide nets hung over the middle – the fourth floor and the seventh and the eleventh. I gave disposable cameras to school kids without much and asked them to document a week of their lives and they asked me why them, and what was so interesting about their lives anyway, and I said, 'It's all interesting. Show me what your room looks like and what you eat for dinner; it is all your rich, real life.' And they gave me back their film and I developed their snapshots of life, and we printed their best photos and framed them and held an exhibition. Then we filmed them seeing themselves differently, somehow.

I loved getting to know that city beyond the postcard high-rises and the giant stone lions outside global banks and the luxe bars and the shopping. The Hong Kong I came to love was complex and nuanced, and the most wonderful blend of grit and modernity.

In my first weeks there, I took photo after photo of bamboo scaffolding, rising impossibly high, each trunk bound to the next with plastic cable ties, thousands upon thousands, crisscrossing the long straight flexible wood. And, when they came down! The shouting of the workmen, high above, dropping bamboo pole after bamboo pole, gravity slamming each perfectly into a waiting truck below, centimetres away from pedestrians and cars and kids, scrambling for space on tiny footpaths.

I watched old men take their pet birds in wooden cages for a walk, smoking and standing around a game of chess played on a permanent stone table in a concrete park. I walked around the outside of a city oasis, barefoot, gingerly placing my soles on rocks of all sizes and shapes – a free foot massage for whoever, whenever. I winced at each step, while old men and old women walked across the same stones, peacefully, calmly.

I zipped down in the subway and I jumped onto minibuses that drove way too fast and I conquered the trams, where you entered through a turnstile from the back and exited out the front. I went to the cinema and found the best Nepalese dumplings in a bar on the second floor of an old crumbling building. From the window, I could look across the street and watch as fit bodies smashed into each other in a makeshift boxing ring.

In among all that, I worked. It was a decent salary, but it was a local one, at a local TV station, so I had none of the expat benefits many other foreigners had: no living allowance, no rental subsidy, no paid trips back home twice a year. I did life like everyone else.

I worked hard and was grateful for whatever came my way. So, when the opportunity came up to be on screen a bit more, I jumped at it. 'Of course,' I said, and I nervously went to the make-up room and wrote my weather script and one night, the newsreaders crossed to me in the studio. There I was, my name and my face on the television, and there was a thrill to it all, that somehow I was going somewhere new and better and different.

I stuck with that for a while, weather and more weather and then finance and sometimes I would read the sport at the desk and then, after about a year, I was asked whether I wanted to read the news, and I said, 'Wow, yes please and thank you so much.' So I started doing that too. I loved it. I felt important.

The shifts were all on a roster and the roster would be put on our desks every second Monday. I'd get into the office, and I would be so excited to see whether my name was on it – for weather or finance or sport, or the main news, I didn't mind which. Anything was a bonus; every shift, every opportunity, I was grateful for.

Slowly, though, things started to change. Not on paper, but in me. About six months into this new world, I noticed myself feeling anxious the Sunday night before the roster came out. And I'd get to work the next morning feeling unsettled, racing to my desk to see that piece of paper that seemed to hold so much power.

I would scan the rows of names and find mine and count how many shifts I had been assigned, and somehow, no matter how many I got, it never seemed enough. I had been happy with just one, even two, a handful of months before. But if I had only four that week and five the next, I would feel like I had been hard done by, or I wasn't good enough, or felt something else uncomfortable and dangerous.

After counting my own shifts, I would look at the other girls' shifts and count theirs too, and I would note how one colleague had ten and another eight and I had only nine, and then they didn't seem like colleagues anymore. There was a thick silent wall between us which we glanced over with smiles and small talk, but we all knew what the others felt.

I started to enjoy my job less. All I really cared about was the next roster. One A4 page, lists of names, numbers of shifts, comparing, comparing, comparing. It was making me sick and one morning, for no reason at all, my body told me that this had to stop. *Enough, Kumi, enough*, it said. And my mind told me to look in the mirror, so I walked into the bathroom and stared at my reflection, and stared deep into my eyes, and said, out loud: Don't you ever let your identity be tied to your job.

And that was it. A switch. An instant shift and change and I felt a weight lift and I hadn't realised how fucking heavy it was. That Monday, I went to work on my train, read my book and looked out the train window at the greenery outside. When I got to work I went to my desk and there was the roster. I counted my shifts and they were about the same as the previous fortnight but this time, they seemed like happy gifts.

I wish I could say that is when everything went up and I never slid back but, like I said, change is like time for me: it goes backwards and forwards and sideways and sometimes I would wonder how I got myself back to a place, abandoning myself yet again.

–

Sara and I would talk about this often – how we go back to patterns we know. I would tell her how I wanted to do things differently, tell my brain new stories about myself. And how it was hard.

She'd always say, matter-of-factly: 'That makes sense. Change is uncomfortable.'

–

In that hospital, where young men went to try to find where they had gone, I asked them a question. What would your business card have said before? Logistics Manager, one said. Specialist, said another. Weapons Technician. Pilot.

And then I asked them, what would your business card say now? I was hoping for, or maybe expecting to hear: Dad, Husband, Son, Gardener, Student. There would always be a pause, their eyes looking into the middle distance. Then, 'My card would say: Ex-Logistics Manager. Ex-Weapons Technician. Ex-Pilot.'

The men wanted to be what they used to be but could never, and would never, be that again.

—

At one place I worked, journalists would make that place their home for decades. They were amazing storytellers, nuanced and fair and brave. They reported on war zones and disasters with an empathetic eye and a heart that ached for humanity. The accolades rolled in – award after award, acknowledgements, praise. And then it would be time for them to leave. Either they had decided to leave or the company had decided, or they had decided together.

In any case, the email would come around. Always three paragraphs. Paragraph one: so and so started working here in (insert date here). Then a few sentences about where they grew up and how they always wanted to tell stories and where they landed their first job.

Second paragraph: a long list of all the places they went to, all the stories they told, all the awards they collected, all the people they mentored and inspired. And something about their personality – hardworking, humble.

Then, paragraph three: how they will be sorely missed, gone but not forgotten, an incredible legacy left behind. Farewells to be had, drinks here, a lunch there. And a thank you.

Several decades, distilled into three paragraphs.

And, come Monday, yes, that person was missed. But life went on. The newsroom still buzzed, someone was in that person's position and grateful for their chance, the speeches had been given and the tears had dried. Business as usual.

For some reason, that's always stuck with me. That at the end of the day, a career can come down to three paragraphs.

–

When I am asked, 'What advice would you give those up-and-coming in the industry?' I give an answer I think no-one wants to hear. What I think they want to hear is: have thick skin; never give up; be grateful; work hard; and if you are not sure how to do something, ask. Don't bitch about your colleagues because one day they might be your boss. Make sure you bring lunch that you can eat with one hand because you will be eating and typing at the same time for most of your career.

But from me, they hear this: you're replaceable.

The moment you realise you are replaceable, that is the moment you are free. Because knowing that someone else can and will come along and do your job – differently, worse, better – you are no longer held hostage by that job. You don't care about up-and-coming 'rivals'. In fact, you welcome new faces and new brains and new hearts.

And each day you still have that job is a good day. The gratitude returns and stays. The fear of what may be, goes, because who knows anyway? You stop fighting to protect your turf; instead, you throw the doors open and welcome others into your space. You tell them, you are great, and you can do this, and let's get you more confident. You give.

And you know, deep down, that if that job goes, you will still be whole. And when that job goes, you will still be you. And by realising this early, I tell them, you hopefully won't have to stress about a roster and count your shifts. And you won't work so hard because your life depends on it, your wellbeing and identity so tied to a persona, that you give everything up to feed that beast, whose appetite never wanes.

No, you will be free, I tell them. And the irony? You will thrive because you won't be gripped by fear.

Home

When Death is Close

The second-last time I saw Dad alive was maybe a year before he died but I really can't be sure. It's embarrassing to admit; a good daughter would know.

Over the years, after the Horsehead Nebula moment, I had seen him maybe a handful of times. Often with years in between. During the six years I lived in Hong Kong, I saw him once – when I came back to introduce my daughter to the family. I'd say we exchanged half a dozen emails or cards in that time.

Then, when I moved back to Australia from that Asian city and re-established life again, Dad just wasn't a priority. It was only in the last four years of him being alive that I saw him regularly. I'd say it was five times, but all quite close together.

I was working in Melbourne on and off, presenting breakfast TV. There, my only focus was work. My alarm would go off at 2:45 am, I would be in the office by 3:30 am. Make-up at 4 am for 45 minutes. Then, an hour to read more briefs, eat some pre-made breakfast like oats and yoghurt, then in the studio at 5:45 am, ready for the camera to roll at exactly 6 am.

It was gruelling and satisfying work. By then, I was drinking decaf coffee, too, so there was no caffeine boost to get me going. At 6 am, with my brain still waking up and feeling a semi-permanent jet lag, the news that day might hand me an interview with the federal Treasurer about some new tax reform, then a switch to an overseas story or an interview about space.

I loved the team effort, the multitude of moving parts, keeping across not only the briefs and interviews but the studio craft – knowing when to turn to a camera, when to pause, when to speak, what tone to speak in. Timing a joke with my co-host, being confident enough to let some of my own personality come through. It was a complex dance and every day was different.

The upside to the early start was that my work for the show was done by around 9.30 am. I would leave the office and try my best to stay awake: a coffee in town, browsing in shops, a grocery stop to get something for dinner that I could make in my serviced apartment. Most days, I would nap for 20 minutes, and 20 minutes only, at 1 pm. Then, at 3 pm, start reading emails and briefs for the following morning, and jump on a production call.

Watch the news at 6 pm. Wind down. Bed at 8:30 pm, hopefully asleep by 9 pm. Then, the next day it would start all over again.

Because of all that lay time during the day, I felt obliged to see Dad each time I was there. It did feel like an obligation, I hate to admit it. I was never excited to see him, I just knew I should. And, I had no excuse: I had time to spare. My flights had been paid for. Later, I would see those work stints as a blessing: time with him in his final years that I never would have made happen myself. We shared no Christmases or birthdays, no regular get-togethers; it just wasn't that kind of relationship. But we had a few hours here and there, and always at his home.

I do remember my lunch with him that day because after it was over I felt panicky and sad and knew he was sick. He had greeted me at the door, still in his dressing gown, even though it was nearly midday. He seemed even smaller and his eyes looked different. Older than old. Glazed over. His walk was slower and he wheezed with every step.

He asked me if I wanted tea. I said I was fine because I didn't want him to do anything, but he said it was important to have tea, so he slowly, ever so slowly, made me one with his thermos hot water and brought it to me with some rice crackers and a mandarin. We sat at his round kitchen table while I ate each wedge and said how nice it was.

I tried to think of things to say. I said the sun was nice, coming in the window, and how cosy and warm his house was. I asked him whether he still watched the Japanese news every morning. He said no, not anymore. I noticed his drinks trolley was dusty and every bottle looked untouched. The label on a half-empty bottle of soda water was peeling off. I felt a tightness build in my throat. I sensed an ending.

I kept drinking my tea, trying to fill some gap between his airless breaths and suddenly he got up and said, 'OK let's go, sushi and cappuccino.' And he went to his bedroom to get dressed and, knowing it would take him a while, I went to the kitchen to take my cup back to the sink, but really, I went into the kitchen to see what was in his pantry and his fridge, to find some clues as to how he might be living.

In the pantry, there were a few packets of instant noodles in the cupboard and packets of green tea and the rice crackers he had given me and some instant coffee. In the fridge, a few pickles and some tofu and milk. There wasn't much at all. He was thin and was wheezing, and I was scared.

He came out of his room. We walked slowly to his car, and he drove slowly to the mall, and it took us double the time to walk to our usual food court. I said nothing about his breathing, and he said nothing. Instead, I told him how nice it was to be back at the mall and how I was looking forward to lunch.

At one point he stopped and put his arm through mine for support, and he leaned in a bit closer. He had never done this before. We had never done this before. His lungs struggled more, and his breath struggled more, and I knew then that my dad was dying. And when we got to the food court, I told him I could get his lunch, and he said thank you, and I asked him what he wanted, and he said he would like a curry with rice. He got his wallet out and gave me $50 and told me to buy my lunch too.

We sat at a white plastic table on white plastic chairs. We didn't say much and he didn't eat much, either. After we finished, I took our plastic trays and half-empty plates to the rubbish area. Then we walked back the way we had come, passing a cupcake shop and a phone repair shop and a one-dollar store with dress-up hats in the window. I pointed out a silly hat and tried to make him laugh.

We had a coffee at a café and sat quietly some more, and then we walked back to the car, every step feeling painful and slow.

I struggled to find any words. Dad drove us back to his house, his laboured breath our soundtrack, and instead of reversing the car into the driveway like he had always done, he drove in forwards because it was easier. When we got out of the car, I noticed the wheels weren't lined up.

—

Granny knew when she was dying. In the last few months of her life, she went in and out of hospital – a dicky heart, she would say. I guess I just thought old people went to hospital, that it was just what they do, and then they come home again and they go in again. I never really thought that one time she was not going to come back home.

Of course, I knew she was getting older, and she knew it too. In the last few years, she started giving away her books, boxes and boxes of them to a second-hand book barn in the country town where we lived. She wrapped up the oldest of old editions of classics for the grandchildren on our birthdays. In the early days of that house of hers, the one she built after my grandfather died, the one where she rebuilt a life on her own and loved it, she would use every room: the dining room for Sunday lunches and the library area for drinks and coffee, the kitchen to cook and then the TV area. The sunroom, where she would sit in a chair and mend socks or clothes, making the most of the afternoon warmth. And then her bedroom, the bed always beautifully made.

But, at around the time her books were packed in boxes and found other homes, she began to use less and less of her space. Her dinners would be on a table in the TV room and then they would be on her lap. Her sunroom became her main room because it was warm for more hours in the day. Her meals became smaller and her pantry less stocked. Some of the garden beds were left to fend for themselves.

And then, her dicky heart took her to hospital more often.

She would stay for a few days. We put her in a nice room on her own. There was a phone in there, but she never used it. She said it was too expensive. Instead, Granny would walk down a few flights of stairs to the public phone, put her coins in and dial our number. Then when she was ready to come home, one of us would pick her up and take her back to her roses and her warm sunny room.

On the hospital stay that would be her last, she was found dead one morning by the nurses. She had been up in the night to go to the bathroom and her dicky heart won that round. She never made it back to her bed. We were told she would have died peacefully. Granny was no more. I was at uni then, and can't remember how I was told, but our dear Granny was gone.

Not long after, we said goodbye to her in a church, even though we were not religious. Afterwards, dozens of us stood on her lawn near the roses that led to the sliding door, to eat sandwiches with the crusts cut off and drink cups of tea. I guess that is what you do. But it felt wrong to be at her home without her there. Granny was her home and her home was Granny. I looked at her garden and wondered who would tend to it now.

I could not articulate it then and it only became apparent later, when family Christmases were not as cohesive anymore, that Granny had been the centre of them all, Granny was the one who we all flocked to. I could not explain how, with her death, I lost her haven. A home where anything was OK, where laughter was paramount, where time could move slowly. Where I could just be.

A few months after she died, we received the final bill from the hospital. This many days, this medication, that intervention. And then, the phone bill. From the private phone in her room, that one she refused to use, instead walking down a few floors to the payphone and using her coins. No, on that final stay, she used that phone and accumulated hundreds of dollars in calls. How strange, everyone said at her wake, I had such a lovely call with your granny just a few days ago. We had not spoken for ages but we had such a long phone call. And we talked all about life.

—

I wasn't quite ready to believe that Dad's life was nearly over. When I got back home, I went into action mode. I decided it was my duty to look after him. Maybe he could move in with me and live in the spare room at the front of the house. Yes, he could sleep there, and he could sit in the courtyard and drink his tea, and he could see my daughter when she came home from school.

It was time to call Dad's doctor, who he'd been with for a long time. Thankfully Dad had been great with paperwork and when he'd retired decades earlier at 55, he'd handed my sister and me a stack of papers – his bank account details, his pension, his superannuation, the names of his doctor and dentist and solicitor. At the time, it'd seemed premature, but gosh it was handy now. When the doctor answered I said, 'I know you can't tell me much, but I am sure Dad is sick.'

And the doctor told me that yes, he couldn't tell me anything, but recommended the next time I see Dad, I ask if we can make an appointment together and I can hear what Dad hears and I can get Dad's permission to see his medical files. I'll do that, I told this stranger.

I was just about to hang up when the doctor jumped in. 'Look,' he told me, 'I can tell you this. Your dad came to see me every year, without fail. But it's been 18 months since I saw him last.' Then he hung up the phone.

—

There is a passage in a favourite book by Cheryl Strayed called *Tiny Beautiful Things,* which comes to me in certain moments. I don't choose the moments but the words stay with me like images and I like to think they are staying with me for a reason.

The part I remember so often is when Strayed's son said to her when he was six, that people die at all ages and we don't know how many years we have. And he said it to her as fact, as much a fact as our sun rising in the east and setting in the west. It just is. And when those words come back to me, it is like his little voice is telling me to know, to deeply know, that what he says is true.

—

At my 21st, Danny played the saxophone. He was the older brother of a uni friend. Danny, who got into some of the world's best music schools. Danny, who named thousands of little musical motifs after colours and plants and feelings, so that when he improvised, he would place those motifs in an order of sorts — *sun* and *blue* and *rain* and *sad*. And those snippets would come together and make a melody. And maybe that melody would never come out in the same way again, because the next time he might play it as *blue* and *sad* and *sun* and *rain*.

Danny, tall and gentle, a few years after playing his saxophone at my 21st, dropped dead on a London street. An aneurysm. One moment alive, the next, without warning, not. Danny, who had become the man of the family when his dad had died. So, when Danny died, that family became not only fatherless, but sonless and brotherless, too.

And I think of another friend, whose mum died when she was 16. We were told about it, our class, all together, underneath a big tree at our school. Years later, that friend came to visit me in Hong Kong. We caught up on decades of life, over a few evenings. And she told me how 33 was a particularly bad age for her. When I asked her why, she said it was because she had been alive longer without her mum than with her mum.

—

My ojiisan died from some lung thing, as far as I know. He had been a smoker. I have a photo of him that I found in Dad's collection – him in his hospital bed, his cheeks drawn. He is wearing a hospital gown and Dad is standing next to his bed on one side and my cousin is standing on the other. Dad would be about 60.

The photo stays with me because, in retrospect at least, it feels like at that moment Dad made a decision, marked in film, like a piece of evidence of a mystery we try to piece together and make sense of. Dad's lapsed doctor's visits, and later, the Hazmat report that indicated there were blood spatters around the bathroom and the laundry sink, the coroner's report indicating lung problems.

Dad must have known what was going to happen to him, and maybe, after seeing his dad wearing a hospital gown, lying in sheets that weren't his own in a bed that sat on linoleum floors, he thought, *That's not going to be me. I want to go out on my terms.*

Amelia

'Hi, my beautiful friend, coming to you live from . . .' That's how pretty much every single message Amelia and I have ever sent to each other has begun. Voice messages, hours upon hours, finding their way across the oceans. 'Coming to you live from my hotel room in DC,' 'Coming to you live from Tokyo.' Or, often, the more mundane, everyday moments: 'Coming to you live from my drive home from work', 'the school run', 'getting groceries'.

I can count on two hands the number of times we have seen each other in person. I could have put that down to geography. She's a journalist too and travels for work and our friendship was formed when she lived overseas. Now we're in the same city, there is no reason to not meet up. But we have never sat at a café and chatted over coffee. In fact, I don't know what her coffee order is.

But I know so much more. So many intricacies, her fears and joys and her soft spots. What makes her laugh, what she likes to eat for lunch at home, what she likes to eat for lunch at work. How she feels about snacks and travel and hotel rooms and airports. Her kids and her partner and her home. We often say, what would we do without each other, without this space, and we both say, I don't know. I would be lost without you, I tell her. And, *how did this friendship even happen.*

It happened like this. Several years ago, I messaged her on Twitter, telling her I liked her story that day, or something about her work. She would message back now and then, and that was it. But then one day I messaged her: *how about we exchange phone numbers.* And we did. And then one day after that, for whatever reason, I left her a voice message.

'I do this with my friend, Linda,' I told her. 'And we like it, it keeps us in touch.' And she left me a short voice message, saying she had never done this before, and how it felt a bit strange, but it was quite fun. She left it from her then home in LA and, immediately, I pictured her in a kitchen, and her living a normal life, and I was somehow part of it. After that, our friendship truly began. And a deep trust in her and the space we were building. 'Hi, my beautiful friend. Coming to you live from':

My morning walk (feeling tired, anxious)

A coffee run (looking forward to the work day, got a great story coming up)

Buying new running shoes (feeling yuck, the body dysmorphia is kicking in)

Changing the sheets on my bed (sorry, this is so boring, but I know you won't mind)

My car (need to download and process something, not sure
how I feel about it)

The car park (in tears, got to wipe my face and get into work,
everything's OK I am just so tired but talking to you has
really helped. Thank you for always being there, my beautiful friend).

One time, I didn't tell her about something that had happened.
For a few days, I kept up appearances. 'Coming to you live
from . . .' – and I told her my news of the day and a few things
that were going on.

But a deep guilt soon set in. I felt like I was lying to her. So I sent
a long voice message, on a morning walk: 'I have kept something
from you, I feel bad about it, it feels wrong, I needed to process it,
I'm feeling terrible, I didn't know how to tell you, I know you won't
judge me, I am sorry for hiding this from you. I feel embarrassed,
humiliated. I think this is what I am going to do.' And of course,
her response was: 'I am so sorry my beautiful friend. I am sorry
this happened. I understand why you didn't tell me at first. There
is nothing to be ashamed of but I would have felt the same.'

How do you explain a friendship that has saved you? And in
a way that is actually what it brings out of you. A space where,
no matter what, you are loved. Where brutal honesty and a
kindness towards your flaws is developed and nurtured, and
where anything is OK. A space where rollercoaster emotions are
welcomed and laughed at and tough, tricky moments can be
worked through, so they don't end up bleeding into other parts
of life. A space where it is not only OK to be, but where you are
expected to be, wonderfully imperfect.

Last Visit

The last time I saw Dad, some months before he died, we had tea at his kitchen table. I was nervous. I had come with two questions: one, how about going to the doctor together. And two, would he consider moving to Sydney.

I asked him about the doctor, trying to keep it casual – more, hey, I was thinking maybe next time you go to the doctor, I could come with you, just to see how everything is. And then I added, wouldn't it be nice if you were in Sydney, there is plenty of room.

Dad looked down and didn't say anything, though I think he heard. The silence went on for maybe a minute. Then he slapped his hands on his thighs, stood up and said, 'OK san Kumi, let's go for sushi and cappuccino.'

–

In what was left of Dad's papers, I found a list of quotes he had written down – in his usual writing, again in pencil. They were about art and simplicity and nature. So similar to ones I would have stuck on a pinboard in my teens and twenties – short, succinct guideposts.

The one that stood out from his selection was from Socrates: An unexamined life is not worth living.

Stargazing

There is a mountain about 500 kilometres north-west of Sydney, where the stars are brighter than bright. Mount Woorut sits on the edge of Warrumbungle National Park – one of only three accredited dark sky places in Australia – where the absence of light pollution means celestial bodies can be studied and monitored, in their purest form.

Here, Siding Spring Observatory usually hosts researchers, who, like most of the native animals in Australia, live a nocturnal existence. They rise with the sunset, and make their way to a telescope – and not one we might imagine, where you put your eye to a lens and look up. No, we are talking tall, round domes, which house mega versions of the backyard types we dabble with.

The researchers stay on-site, in sparse yet comfortable rooms, in a two-storey brick block. Each room has a bed and a desk, built-in wardrobes, and a bathroom. There is a shared kitchen and dining area, a living space with a few board games and a television.

Every window has the thickest of thick blackout blinds, because no light from inside is allowed to bleed out into the darkness. It can ruin what the telescopes researchers are trying to see.

In the two years after Dad died, this secluded place became my home – for a week each time. I was part of a huge live TV production called *Stargazing Live* – a documentary series where, over three consecutive nights in winter 2017 and 2018, we broadcast the wonders of our universe from Siding Spring Observatory. I was one of a handful of presenters. I am not sure how I got the gig – (no-one asked me how, strangely, so no diversity chats were needed) – but I devoured every second of it and knew, even at the time, that I was part of something special.

Leading the converge was English physicist Professor Brian Cox and Australian host, Julia Zemiro. Just having Brian and his brain there made it all seem surreal. With him was a team from the BBC, and then we had a huge crew from the ABC – providing all the cables and outside broadcast trucks and site crew and runners. It was a massive production.

Think of it like this: live television requires studios and antennas and solid wiring and electrics. Sound-proof spaces and lights and cameras and audio technicians. We decided to do all that – on the top of a mountain, across multiple sites. Basically, creating a series of TV studios, from scratch, and having it all go to air – live. Purely on a technical level, it was an incredible undertaking.

The main presenters' studio was inside one of the telescopes, in an atrium-like area. It was necessarily cold so the equipment could operate. Brian and Julia often wore gloves and coats on-air. My 'studio' was the Dark Field – the highest point at the observatory, about one kilometre up a dusty road from the main site. Cold, windy and exhilarating. My role was to co-present three segments a night, so nine in total, with the wonderful, white-bearded astronomer Greg Quicke. A self-taught lover of the skies, he had a way of communicating complex science to everyone.

I loved that mountain. I loved my room. I loved everything about the long days we spent together. A bubble of creativity and camaraderie. No shops or distractions. I have a photo from that time that would look like nothing much to most, and understandably so. It's taken from my perspective, sitting in our makeshift meeting room. My script is in front of me, Brian and the rest of the presenters are sitting around the table, various science brains and producers. We're hashing out the script for the night to come. It's my idea of work heaven: a mix of brains and expertise, a shared love of a topic, and a passion for creating live events.

And once we arrived at our mountain and settled into our rooms, we stayed there. At the end of long rehearsal days, before our three nights on air, the majority of the crew would bus down the road and into the nearest town, Coonabarabran. A handful of us got to stay in the rooms on-site. Our names were printed on A4 paper and were stuck on the outside of our doors.

There were strict rules, mainly around light, at night. We could not leave doors open for long, so when we went in and out of the shared common area, or our bedrooms, we had to open and close them quickly, so the light would not escape. We could not use torches to walk around in the darkness either, they were too bright. So we all brought headlamps so we could shuffle from place to place. And those had to have red lights, so the glare was not too bright.

Each evening, I would look up at those stars. They were so close to me, so much closer than they had ever been before. Their brightness was endless and with each minute of my eyes adjusting to the darkness, another layer of their magic would be revealed. It was one of the most special times of my life and there were moments that I thought about Dad and how much he would have loved to see them. I wished I could have brought him with me. Or, at least, that I could have been able to tell him about it all.

—

Despite that night sky, my favourite time of day was the morning. I would wake up and head to the kitchen and make myself break-fast. In that room, there would often be someone, or no-one, from our small mountain cohort, also doing the same thing. We usually kept quiet, everyone in their own worlds, keeping in touch with family through text messages or a quick, hushed phone call, or attending to life admin. It was also about energy preservation. The days were long: scripting and rehearsals and more rehearsals. Then meetings and a dress rehearsal and then the actual live broadcast, which of course had to be quite late at night so the skies were as dark as they could be.

So, those mornings were my peaceful space, where the mountain was inhabited by only a few of us. After breakfast, I would make a small plunger of coffee. And instead of drinking it in the kitchen, I would take it and a cup to a patch of red dirt outside. I'd balance the plunger in a tuft of grass and pour myself one cup, then another, telling myself that somehow, all that I had done and undone, all that I had wanted and avoided, had led me to his moment. And that I may never come back here again. I could not have wanted for anything else.

Years after those broadcasts, I would email the people running the observatory, and ask whether it would be possible to come and stay again. I wanted to write there, run there, see that sky again. I wanted that simplicity and that connection to the vastness. I was never able to make it happen – though I still might. But, if I were to go back, there would be no broadcast and no camaraderie and no shared sense of achievement; no WhatsApp group chats where my BBC colleagues would share their scary-Australian-animal-of-the-day photo (usually a big spider); no learning from others with brains so much smarter than mine. So many things would be missing.

–

Seven years after our broadcasts from that mountain, Greg Quicke died. Because of his white beard, and because when he and I broadcast from our windy outpost, it would fly around, he was given the name Space Gandalf by countless viewers. Space Gandalf is who he became and he had a wonderful chapter of life as that person – filming specials and spreading his message even further. So often in my industry I had seen others get a boost of new-found recognition, and they would change. Become addicted to a new status. But Greg's soul never shifted. He was still the happiest when walking in remote parts of his Australia – the dusty desert in Western Australia, under the sky he loved.

When I heard he had died, those of us who had worked with him up the mountain – (and, that day, the sharing of sadness with those from that time – *Have you heard?*) – I remembered what he had said to me one evening, back when we were doing a dress rehearsal for that night's broadcast. I had been trying to memorise every fact, in order. My brain was getting scrambled. I was starting to feel inadequate, and wondering whether I would get it all right later that evening.

We downed tools for a moment to take a breather. Just ask me questions, he told me. So I did. I asked him why this and why that, and if because of this, then why that. Stars and space and planets and light and sun. And I could feel my worry dissipating with every question and every answer – that, in fact, my curiosity was enough. From that, the rest would follow.

Greg could see the shift. He smiled at me and said, his blue eyes shining: 'You got it. You don't have to worry.'

A Final Journey

I haven't told you what happened to Dad next, after the Hazmat crew came and went. We were told he needed to be cremated soon and that the coroner would only hold onto his body for a short time, so my sister and I found a place that would pick up Dad's body and drive it to the crematorium. I wasn't there when it happened.

We found the place online and it was much cheaper than the one Dad's lawyer recommended – the lawyer who seemed to think Dad's bank account was his own. It felt wrong to be doing it all remotely, telling the company that, no, there won't be anyone there, no family, no friends. Just, if you could pick up the body and take it to the crematorium and let me know when he is due to be cremated and yes, I am his daughter, but I am interstate and this is what he would have wanted anyway.

My sister and I had a lot to do on other fronts. We had to get his death certificate, sell his car, work out what to do with his house, bank accounts and super, pay the lawyer and also pay thousands to the clean-up crew. At the same time, we were working and looking after our kids. Interestingly, our different personalities really came to the fore: she was so much better at some tasks, like the car and the logistics; I, to my surprise, was better at holding the lawyers accountable. And, when it came to the moment we had to open the door to his house, I was the one who went in first.

What was it that Christopher Hitchens said? I am sure I heard this in an interview, one of his long, intellectually swirling chats. It was something along the lines of: the greatest strength of humans is that we can rationalise anything. And the greatest weakness of humans is that we can rationalise anything. I told myself that sending Dad off in the way that we did was fine, but the reasons I did it that way caught up with me and I felt immense guilt and shame. And I knew that because I didn't want to tell anyone about it.

Dad's body went to a place in Dandenong, outside Melbourne's CBD, although I recorded it in my head as the Dandenongs, the range of mountains further away, where winding roads weave their way through lush native forest. Dad drove us there some-times, as kids, switching off the car engine and letting it roll down a hill.

What I remember most, though, was when he would stop the car on the side of the road near some native ferns. We would all get out, and he would show us the ferns and pick some. I would worry that we were doing something illegal, because it was a national park, but I knew not to question him, and he just picked the ferns and put them in the car.

He was the man who boiled water once a day and put the rest in a flask and put that flask in the boot of his car and he would take that flask to golf and the shops and could make a cup of tea whenever he wanted.

The ferns are good for pickling, he said. And many years later, when he told the story of when he was a child sent to the mountains outside Tokyo and given the piece of A4 paper with plants drawn on it, I thought maybe some things never leave us. But at the time, I had been embarrassed and when other cars passed, I had wondered what the people inside were saying about us and I just wanted him to pick those damn ferns quickly so we could get back in the car and I could shrink away. I had wished I had any other father, not this one. I hated the way he combed one strand of hair over his bald head and I hated his stained teeth and I hated the way he spoke such broken English and I hated how no-one could understand him. And I had wished those trips to be over.

And then on the final morning at Dad's place, I would pack my suitcase and start to feel sad. I would see the sofa bed pulled out with our sheets still on it, and think that tonight it would just be a sofa again. All back to normal for Dad, too. I would see his typewriter and the deck of cards and the glass full of shells that we would use as betting tokens and his harmonica and the little pet rock, and I would forget the moments I wished he was like the other dads, standing on the sidelines while I played hockey and taking me to the movies and telling me that everything was going to be OK.

And then he would drive us to the bus station or the train station or the airport, whichever mode of transport was the one for that holiday, and then we would wave goodbye, and I would think he was going to be lonely but above all, I wished that I could have been better, nicer.

—

In the years following Dad's death, I would sometimes think of the onigiri, the rice balls, the ones I thought were embarrassing. I would picture him making them the night before, wrapping them carefully so they wouldn't get damaged, storing them in an Esky and planning out our meals. And I would remember how I felt on the boat and how I wished for normal food like the normal kids and I would feel ashamed and spoilt and ungrateful decades after the fact, and wondered whether he thought I was spoilt and ungrateful too.

—

More things I discovered about Dad. He never told me about them when he was alive, and why would he. In his paperwork, in the smallest things that remained of his life, were three letters.

One congratulating him on becoming an official translator. He must have applied and done some tests. I wondered what for, to be a translator for Japanese people? For the courts or the police or in schools? All I knew is that he had wanted this, he got it, he kept the letter and in his wallet was a laminated card with his face on it.

The second, a letter from Salvation Army, thanking him for his regular donations. And that is where my knowledge stopped, too. I wanted to know more – how did he come across them and why did he donate? How much and how often, and what made him want to give away the money, of which he had little?

And the third was a letter from a children's home, also grateful for his donations. This one got to me. How did he find it? It was one in a local area, not a big organisation with advertising campaigns. Not a well-known place. But, somehow, he had found it, or it had found him, and he gave them money. Kids with no families, children with no parents. I could see why he did that. Forever a little boy in the mountains.

I wish I had asked him about that home. About those children. Whether he met any of them. How he donated the money. Was it by cheque? Maybe I would have told him that I, too, have a deep wound in my body that aches for children who are not wanted and alone. And how I would love to adopt and if I had all the money in the world, every child would feel safe and loved.

Maybe I would have told him about the first charity I donated to when I was 14, a guide dog organisation, and how my small amount of money per month went to helping train a small puppy so it could be the eyes for a human. Or maybe I would have told him about my sponsor child from Rwanda, who, in his photo on the website, was wearing a pink T-shirt with the word 'Love' on the front. And how in photos years after, despite the fact he had grown and was learning to read and enjoying soccer, he was wearing the same pink T-shirt.

Even if I had told him, I wonder what he would have said. I suspect he would have listened, paused, and then said: 'San Kumi, let's get sushi and cappuccino.'

Who Said Goodbye?

A year after Dad was cremated, I decided I wanted to see where it had happened, where we had sent him. I had pictured what was left of Dad's body being driven through the Dandenong Ranges, along those winding roads through lush green, maybe even going past the ferns he liked to pick.

I flew to Melbourne and picked up a hire car, and it was then that I realised the place he went to – the place I sent him to – wasn't in the mountains, it wasn't past ferns and lush greenery. It was off a highway and past an industrial area on the outskirts of the city: a memorial park with big stone gates at the entrance, etched with the words 'Celebrating Life'.

Dad had come here on his own in an unadorned box and on his paperwork read *unattended cremation*. I am here now, Dad, I wanted to tell him. I have come to see where I sent you. But it all felt too late. I sat in my parked car for a few minutes, looking at a group of women going through the entrance together. I waited for them to pass, my shame so deep I thought if they saw me, they would know my truth, somehow know that my body carried itself in a way that only the guilty know.

I felt shame as I walked up the concrete path to the café, past eucalypts and inscriptions of love and life and family and death and new beginnings. I felt shame as I sat in the corner of the café, waiting for a stranger called Debra who worked at the memorial park. I had contacted her a few months before, asking if I could visit and see where Dad had gone, see where he had been cremated. Absolutely, she said. You are most welcome.

Debra was kind over email and kinder in person, and as soon as I met her, I thought, *This will be OK. I will be OK. I am OK.* I told her about how I hadn't been there for Dad, how I left him on his own – a confession really. She listened and told me how every family does things differently and, in a lifetime, we might prepare only one or two funerals so really, how are we meant to know? Her eyes told me: you did what you could at the time.

And then she showed me around the park. It was really lovely – simple, peaceful. Native birds nourishing themselves on native flowers. Solitary people wandering through small gardens or sitting on a stone bench. Flowers left on small rectangular name plates, embedded gently in the green grass. Dad would have loved it here, I told Debra. I texted the same thing to my sister as I wandered around, along with the reassurance I needed for myself: *We chose well.*

And then we paused near a concrete building with ladders going up to the roof and Debra asked me whether I was up to seeing the crematorium and I said yes, I want to understand the process. We went into a room where a floor-to-ceiling glass wall showed the cremation area, and we sat in chairs lined up in rows to give mourners a view inside. Beyond the glass were big ovens and I just sat there and looked and I said nothing and she said nothing because she knew this part, where we have to be given time to sit and contemplate.

A few minutes later, she pulled out a few sheets of paper from a folder she must have been carrying. On one piece of paper, an order of release from the coroner's office. On another, Dad's arrival at the park and a record of his coffin being checked against a number that had been assigned to him. Basically, it was a form to confirm the right body is being received.

What would have happened then, I asked her. Who took care of him? Did they say anything to him?

She told me that Dad's coffin would have been loaded onto a trolley and a man called Dan looked after him that day. She said that she had contacted Dan and asked him if there are any rituals he follows when he has a body, and Dan told her that he always places his hand on a coffin and tries to think of the person inside so they can be sent off by another human being. So it was Dan who said goodbye to my dad.

And from there, Dad was taken through the first chamber and his cremation started at 11:35 am. His remains were removed two and a half hours later and I told her that seems like a long time. She said that it takes a while for everything to evaporate – clothing, the coffin – and in that time, everything goes back to bone.

Dad's bones would have gone into the second chamber to cool down and then the bones ground to ash and that was how Dad ended up, in a small pot, mailed to my sister a week or so later.

I told Debra I didn't know what we would do with the ashes. She replied there was no need to rush. But I knew what Dad wanted. Or what he didn't want.

In his will, he said he wanted his ashes to be scattered on Australian soil. *I express my clear wish*, he wrote, *that neither my body nor my ashes be returned to Japan.*

–

Debra didn't start out in this job. At 18, she was an undercover police officer in Melbourne. Not long after she started, a bomb went off outside the headquarters where she was based. Russell Street. The bomb was hidden inside a car. One female police officer later died from her injuries, and it could have been Debra too. She told me that afterwards she remembered sitting inside headquarters and being blasted across the room; later, when the investigation was going on, she remembered something else.

The day before the bombing, a piece of chipboard was put over the window her desk was under – a coincidence, a fluke. Without it, Debra could have been badly injured or even died. This would haunt her for years. Why was she spared? Why did she escape unscathed? At such a young age, she learned to ask serious questions of life.

An Address in Tokyo

It took two trips to Japan to find my dad's home, the one I used to visit as a kid. Dad had died a few years earlier. The first year was taken up with the admin of death, including the tidying of his home and the selling of his home. One morning, we closed the door on Unit 142 and handed over his keys to the retirement village.

After that first year and after his birthday came and went, I had time and space to breathe and think about what was next. One of the few things that survived his death was a small black notebook. It was handmade, with rough staples on the top. Inside were rectangular pages that appeared to have been cut from old A4 paper – on the back were words and sentences that looked like they had been written a long time ago.

Inside the book were addresses, many of them typed on Dad's typewriter. There was an old address of mine from many years earlier, with multiple handwritten amendments over the top of the original, and towards the back of the book there were even more of my addresses in my own writing. He must have cut them out from the back of envelopes I sent him. No wonder he thought I was living on a park bench at times: there, in his notebook, was the evidence of my failed chapters and old homes and new homes. I wished there was perhaps only one address, like those people who just have it all together and build their home and stay there.

There were other addresses, too, my sister's and my mum's, and then there was one that said Family Home, which I guessed was his parents', my obaasan and ojiisan. There were a few names I didn't recognise and a few I thought might be his brothers, which Mum confirmed.

The eldest brother was perhaps alive somewhere in the north of Japan, living a life as a dead man. I got a friend to call the number of Dad's other brother and was told he was going into hospital for an operation and was a bit deaf, so it was hard to find out where he was. I wanted to find some family. It felt wrong that no-one knew my dad had died.

My only hope was the family home. In that home, I hoped to find my cool cousin, the eldest son of my eldest uncle, who had driven his dad north and who drove us around the streets when we were kids. The reason I thought he might still be there was because Dad had left it to him: when Dad's parents died, Dad could have gone back to Japan to live in the house, but he decided the best thing was for my cousin to have it. After all, he was the one who had been left in debt because of his father; he was the one who needed it the most. So Dad stayed in Australia, and my cousin – I assumed – stayed in my grandparents' house.

I remember being shocked when I found out that Dad visited his home country only three times after he moved to Australia. Once for a work trip; the other times, to see his each of his dying parents. 'When my father died, my family died,' he said. 'When my mother died, my country died.' After his mother's death, Dad felt Japan was no more.

One morning, I set out from my hotel in Tokyo, the one with the winding paths in the garden, and walked down the steep hill towards the subway. I made my way to an address I had never gone to on my own before. It felt like a long way, over a dozen stops. Sitting next to me was an older woman with a brown winter hat on, her hands neatly placed in her lap. I could feel her watching me as I wrote in my notebook.

Hidari kiki? she asked me. *Left-handed?*

I am, and I hated it as a kid. My family would joke about me being unable to use scissors, and my hand would always smudge my writing and get jammed in the spirals of notebooks. I also knew it was frowned upon in Japan, and I was told that had I been brought up there, I would have had to change to being right-handed.

So, I apologetically said to the woman, yes, left-handed.

That's good, she replied, smiling.

The woman would have been around Dad's age, had he still been alive. I looked at her face and studied her wrinkles and the shape of her eyes and I realised I missed that shape. The shape that I covered with sunglasses but which, when I saw it on others, looked familiar and felt comforting and I couldn't remember the last time I saw an old, wise Japanese face so close to me.

She turned to me again. *Haafu?* she asked. Half?

Again, it wasn't the best of terms, to be half. Something else to apologise for. And I did, for my Japanese. I told her I spoke very little and I was sorry, and yes I was a haafu, and I told her that my mum was Australian and my dad was Japanese. She smiled and repeated, That's good.

And, before she left the train, she looked at me one more time. *Ima* – ima meaning now – Now, we say double. We don't say half. You are double.

—

I found out more about Dad after he died from newspaper clippings he left behind. They survived the Hazmat cull; they must have been in an outer room, away from his single bed where his body lay unnoticed. Most of the articles were in Japanese but I could make out vague categories: environment, politics, quite a lot on the White Australia Policy.

The folders were those old-style suspension files that would have hung in a metal filing cabinet, with metal hooks at each end. When I thumbed through what had interested him, what had made his brain tick, I remembered doing the same thing myself: cutting out articles, filing them away in folders, categorising. For a second, I felt a wave of nostalgia for a relationship that never existed but could have – a daughter cutting out words from a newspaper, a dad telling her how he still does the same thing. A chat over a cup of tea about where each person's interests overlapped.

In those folders, too, I found articles Dad had written. Some were in English; most were in Japanese. I knew those were his, though, because his face was next to the headlines, or I could see his name written in kanji. Taguchi Akira. The TA – imagine a square, cut into four. Then GUCHI – imagine an open box. Then AKIRA – the symbols for sun and moon. *The light coming from the sun. Brightness.* Symmetrical. Certain. 田口 明. His name always looked so good in print.

Of course, what he chose to write about was even more interesting than what he had collected. What had he really been interested in? What had he fought for? I could read some parts, and the photographs helped. Pollution in Tokyo Bay from his days at *The Asahi Shimbun* newspaper, before he came to Australia. A reflection on the Bombing of Darwin. One on the Australian bicentenary. Another on multiculturalism. One on Australia Day. Another on the RSL clubs and the men who drank there. Another on the White Australia Policy and when it ended – 1973, the year before Dad came to Australia. The first wave of migrants post–World War II. During the war, people of Japanese origin were interned as 'enemy aliens'.

Not so different from me, I wanted to tell him. Me, not so different from you.

–

I got off the train and exited the station onto a busy road with a banner of a fish hung high, stretching over the four lanes of traffic. I followed my map down one long street and then another, and wove my way around a park where kids were playing on swings. The streets were peaceful and clean and the sounds of life gentle.

I turned left and right and left again, wondering whether I was lost. Nothing looked familiar. Nothing felt familiar.

But then, just one turn later, I knew. My body had memories here, ones my mind had forgotten. I was close to home. I had seen these streets in photos, me and my sister walking in the middle, holding shopping bags. Yes, these were the alleys my cousin drove us around in his bucket-seat car. I knew it. I felt it.

I kept walking, past a rice ball shop and a pharmacy and a store with everything you could imagine: washing liquid and tools and flowers and boxes of tissues, all laid out neatly in rows with bright fluorescent lighting overhead. The shops sat right on the street, no steps up, and very few had doors, just open frontages, shuttered at night with garage-like doors.

I kept following my map and within a few blocks had found the address of my grandparents' home, and I looked around for a house but there was just a two-storey red-brick building. At the bottom was a clothes shop, and on the top, a series of small apartments. I snuck up an external flight of stairs to check out the apartments.

Maybe the house had been sold, I thought, and in its place, these shops were built. This was the place. The address was stamped on the brick in brass, and in my patchy Japanese I asked the woman in the clothes shop, 'This is your address, right?' as I pointed to it on my map. Yes, she said, this is it.

Even though the address was correct, the building was not. I was looking for the home I remembered in my mind, with a balcony and a front door. Not a clothes shop made of red bricks. I went over the road and into a café that was lined with vinyl and I ordered an iced coffee and a toasted sandwich. I sat with old men who smoked and tried to figure out my next move. I was relieved, in one sense, because I had not thought through what I was actually going to do if I did find the house. But I was surprisingly sad. My house, the house, our family house, was gone.

I tore out a page from my notebook and fashioned it into a square and folded a paper crane. I took a photo of it on the café table, then a photo of it resting in my hands, and I told the crane that it had another job to do now. And I stood and left the café and walked over the road, and I rested the little crane on the plaque of the building that had the address of what had been my grandparents' home. I told it to look after the building, and I walked away.

—

But I *knew* I was in the right place. The only way I know how to explain that feeling where your body knows something your mind doesn't, is in relation to tuning a violin.

The way I was taught from very young was that I would tune my A string, either from a tuning fork or from a piano, and once that string was in tune, I would tune the next string to be a perfect fifth below: five notes difference. And then I would tune the string below that, another perfect fifth, and finally the highest string, a perfect fifth above the original A.

I had to get it exact. Most of the time I was pretty accurate, but towards the latter part of my violin days, I had a teacher called Josette who scared me more than the others. She was French, bold and bosomy, and I would see her once every two weeks for an hour and a half of relentless discipline.

Your tuning is not great, she would tell me, and we would spend the first 15 minutes of my lesson getting it right. You're only *listening* to the notes, she told me. You have to *feel* them. Stop thinking, start feeling, she'd say in her rich accent.

Josette told me I had to feel for the vibrations as I played two strings together, instead of hearing whether they were in tune with each other. Play together, she would shout, and *feel*. And I would play them together and try to make them feel and try to make myself feel. But I couldn't get it – until I did. I felt the notes vibrating together, a pulsing through the air, waves dancing together, perfectly in sync.

If you don't feel the notes *dancing* together, you are not in tune! Again!

So we would do it again and again and again, and I learned the dance of two notes and how the most minute adjustment was the difference between being audibly in tune and really in tune, and I would wait until I felt the pulse, and I would wait for her to smile as much as a smile would appear on her face, and then she would say, Good, now we can begin.

That is how my body felt when it turned that corner onto the street lined with shops, near my grandparents' house. It was as if my particles and the air around them became one; the inside of my body and the outside world were the same. It was an invisible dance, and I felt at peace, I felt at home, and I realised I had known this feeling more than once before.

On the streets of Moscow; the first time I walked onto my university campus; those moments when, on a run, everything seemed to come together and felt just right and I would put my arms up in the air and know that this precious moment was one that may not come again. A feeling that the air and the dirt and the sounds and the light and the colours were all coming together, perfectly timed. And my body, just one part of the mystery.

Lost and Found

When I was eight, my first friend at a new primary school was a girl called Tanya and she wore her long dark hair in plaits, one on each side of her smiley face. I was drawn to her from the beginning; maybe she was to me too, and we were similar, in a way. Her dad was Chinese and her mum was Australian, so we had the half thing going on.

Her home often became my home. Her dad was a doctor, and he had an office that we were sometimes allowed to go into and on his shelves were rows of VHS tapes, movies galore. *Star Wars* and *Raiders of the Lost Ark* and names and places I had never heard of and it was paradise. We would settle in on the big lounge in the sitting room and eat snacks and watch movies and play with her Burmese cat.

One holiday, we went to her Australian grandparents' place, a few hours' drive away, on a bush block. Their house was brick and surrounded by gum trees and we ambled around there, eating food and running around in the trees outside. It was dry and the cicadas would shriek and sometimes there would be wombats.

We loved running around outside and on a late afternoon, we raced out the back door and into the scrub below and pretended to live off the land. We hunted and foraged for berries and leaves and made up stories about what we were going to use them for.

We were having so much fun, we didn't notice the sun go down. By the time the shadows had long gone, we looked around and everything was dark and the back of the house, which should have been lit up, had disappeared. We looked around again and realised we were lost. But we thought we hadn't gone too far. I think the house is this way, one of us would say. Yes, that way. And we would walk a bit and push through scrub . . . but there was no house.

No, maybe it was that way, the other said. And we would turn back from where we had come and push back through and think that yes, this time was right, but after a few minutes everything looked unfamiliar again. After doing this a few times, I started to feel panicky. And we said, maybe we are lost, and then it started to feel worse and more real and the darkness became darker.

We wanted to get back, it was cold and I started picturing the warm kitchen and the yellow light and dinner being served and I just wanted to be back there, safe. We tried again; surely the back of the house is that way, one of us said. We turned around and we saw some lights, quite far away.

It was the house, in a totally different place to where it had been before, as if it had been lifted up and spun around and plonked back on the dirt. But it hadn't moved, only we had. I felt silly for getting lost and silly for getting panicked and silly for not realising how far we had gone. And scared that it didn't seem to take much to lose something so solid. Just one turn here, another one there, then throw in a slight distraction and – lost.

Just one spin back the other way, or admitting that maybe your brain isn't seeing things clearly, and there, there are the lights on the porch, yellow light glowing. You head back and enter to find food on the table and laughter and chatter and safety. All it took was seeing things a different way and – found.

A Familiar Balcony

I wanted to find my dad's home. It still bothered me that none of Dad's family knew he was dead. I kept thinking of the crane I'd left on the building that wasn't the home he knew or the home I knew as a child, wasn't where my grandparents had lived.

Surely that house wasn't gone. I still had a little bit of hope that maybe I'd got something wrong with the address. The shop that I had visited was too established to have been built on the land on my grandparents' home. It looked like a place I would have seen as a child. I also didn't remember their home having been in the main shopping area.

As it happened, my work at the time was on an ABC TV show called *Compass,* where we made films about science and art and religion and philosophy. All the meaty stuff. My story fitted the brief: the story of me not knowing where I belonged, the story of where my home was, the story of my dad dying and me trying to find where my grandparents had lived. I reluctantly agreed to become the story – after all, my work is to tell the stories of others. I just wasn't sure I was a compelling subject. Yet I could sense that there was something universal in the idea, and the fact that it was a challenging prospect made me feel like it was important to do.

We set off in March 2019 – my producer Tracey, camera operator Richard, and me. We filmed me arriving in Japan and going to the place I had stayed since I was a child, and we filmed me walking through that garden. We filmed the streets I knew. And, we set out to try to find my grandparents' house. For this part, I enlisted the help of a dear friend Melanie's son, Shoma, who is also a halfie like me: Aussie mum, Japanese dad. He is bilingual – he is more Japanese in nature but can tap into the Australian way of doing things.

I needed his language skills to help me solve the mystery. I needed him to talk to people, ask around about the house, maybe even look up housing records. My reliance on Google Maps and scattered memories only got me so far. On my first morning in Tokyo, Tracey and Richard and I met Shoma for a coffee. I showed Shoma my dad's notebook where he'd written his family home address and we discussed our plan.

The next morning we met near the address where the home used to be. Shoma told me that he had checked the housing records and there was nothing to indicate that the home was gone. We then went to the building that I had found a year before. The shopkeeper there said the same thing: Yes, this is the address.

Same outcome. I had hoped for something different now that I had Shoma's language skills on my side. I didn't want to leave, we didn't want to leave, so we went to regroup over the road and sat in the same café I'd sat in a year earlier, the one where I made the paper crane.

I told Shoma that I'd thought we might learn something new and that maybe the fact I couldn't speak fluent Japanese had been the barrier. I wonder what happened, he replied. At some point I mentioned my surname. An old man who was smoking at the back of the shop piped up, 'Taguchi?' He came up to us and asked us what we were doing. Shoma explained.

'I knew them,' the old man told us. 'Yes, they ran the hardware shop. It was big – they were successful and then, you know, the son . . .' He meant the son, my uncle, who gambled away the money, the one who had to be driven north, the one who was dead to the family. 'Well, they had to sell some of the hardware shop and it was smaller. I remember when they renovated their house they gave away a lot of things and I got a few of their zabuton (the large flat cushions for the floor). They were very nice people.'

The significance of this moment hit me. He was talking about my family. My grandparents. On this street. Their shop. I'd never heard anyone other than my parents speak of them. For the first time in my life, I was somewhere my family was known. Where my place was known – where *I* was known. I choked up and kept blinking to get rid of the tears because they felt irrational. By this stage, Richard had picked up his camera and started rolling, he could tell something was going on. So, for the audience, for our film, I recounted what had happened in the last few minutes. Then I asked the old man, through Shoma, 'Do you know what happened to their house? My grandparents' house?'

He said, 'Ah, their house. Yes, it is here.' Dumbfounded, I asked, 'What? Here?' He repeated, 'Yes, here. I can show you.' And he shuffled across the road, pointing to a side gate near the shop I had been going to, the address in the book my dad had kept. We followed the old man through the gate and he said, 'See, here: Taguchi.' He pointed to my family name on a wooden sign on the gate. I said, 'Yes: this is it, this was where we came.'

And then I saw the house beyond the gate. Two storeys with a white facade. It was the same but different. The same aspect, the same balcony on the second level, but it looked newer than I remembered. When Japanese people renovate their homes it's not how we might do it in the west – repainting, removing a wall, putting in carpet, changing the lighting. The Japanese tear down the home entirely and rebuild it. The inside will be different but they often keep the outside similar to how it was before. They must have done this. But it was the house, the home. It was still there.

The old man was racing up to the front door, and we stopped him. That was for later. I wasn't ready. Now that the home was there, now that it was most likely that my cousin was still living in it, I wasn't prepared for what to do next. It is a strange thing, to knock on a door and wonder who might open it; to ask them, 'Do you know Akira? Do you remember me? I am his daughter. I *was* his daughter – he is dead.'

—

Once my sister and I die, our Taguchi name will die with us. None of our children has it. (Her kids have it as a first surname, more like a middle name than a double-barrelled surname.)

248

It'll continue in Japan for a while at least, given Dad was one of three sons and all of them had sons, too. But here in Australia, my family's Taguchi will cease to exist.

—

Around the same time that movie came out where the woman flung ping-pong balls out of her vagina, the Tamagotchi toy came out – a little electronic pet that was housed inside an egg-shaped plastic watch. You had to feed it and keep it alive. It was quite funny, apparently, back then, to call me Kumi Tamagotchi. And every time it happened, I smiled or laughed. As if it was the first time I had ever heard the joke.

—

On most of my childhood visits to Japan, we would go to Kiddy Land – a multistorey toy shop where you could buy anything imaginable. They had a whole floor of pens and paper, another floor of just stuffed toys. It was paradise. We were allowed to choose one thing.

Once, I got a soft toy – I picked up a little cat and then changed my mind, and chose a bear instead. Then, at the counter, I thought about the little cat and how I had held it and hugged it and felt guilty that I had told it that it was coming home with me. I begged Mum to let me swap, but we were in a rush so I had to leave the little cat behind. For weeks afterwards, I whispered to the sky, I am sorry, someone will come and buy you.

Another time, I bought a Hello Kitty calculator. I still have it and it still works, 40 years on. What's so great about it is that the keys are not square buttons with the numbers on them – the shape of the number is the key. The button for 1 is shaped like a 1, and you press the whole number down. The 2 shaped like a 2. The calculator itself is solar-powered, and shaped like a cat — you push the cat's head upwards to reveal the calculator screen.

But the best thing was, on that same trip, I found stickers with my name on them. You know those shops where you rotate display racks of cups and keyrings and hats to see if your name is there? In Australia, there was always Anna and Rachel and Sophie and Ben and Matt and Sam, but never Kumi. In Japan, though, I could find my name everywhere. It felt both special (to find them), and strange (to know my name was quite common). There it was, on stamps and stickers and pens. I bought a pack of stickers, and I carefully placed a few on the back of my Hello Kitty calculator, as if to say, See, see my name? It's not made up. It's real.

—

We went back to the café. I was elated and scared. The old man was having the time of his life and proceeded to tell us that the man who ran the senbei shop next door also knew my grandparents. So we all went to the shop and the old man explained to the perturbed young couple in charge that this was a TV crew from Australia and I was a Taguchi.

The young man cooking rice cakes on a small grill said he didn't know a Taguchi but maybe his dad would. He picked up the phone and made a call and within a few minutes, another old man emerged. His hair was roughly dyed black. He walked down the stairs behind the shop counter and the first old man repeated the story about the Taguchis. You know, the ones who

250

had the hardware shop, and then lost a lot of the hardware shop because of, you know, the eldest son.

And the second old man said, Ah yes, I knew them, and then he went out the back for a few minutes, and when he returned, he had an old phone book in his hands. The phone book, he told us, was from the time my grandparents had their shop, and he opened it up and he pointed to a page that showed all the shops in a row, just the floorplans, to indicate which shop was where. That was the hardware shop, he said, and see there? That is their name. Taguchi. Yes, that was their shop.

I asked Shoma to ask him what my grandparents were like. Your grandfather was quiet, he told us. But I remember he was hardworking. And very kind.

My family was known in a café and we were known in a phone book and the Taguchi name was on a humble sign on a gate at the back of a shop. A name that I had so wished wasn't mine, for so many decades of my life, finally had a place.

—

We had to decide what to do. The first step was to see who lived in the house. It was mid-afternoon by this stage, and I figured if my cousin did still live there, his wife would be the only one at home.

We just have to knock on the door, I told Shoma, hoping he would say it was too rude and intrusive, we couldn't possibly. Then I could just leave a note, much like a paper crane. *Hi, I am here but hey, if you don't want to talk, that's OK.* But Shoma thought it was OK to knock on the door, so we did. I wanted the camera far away; it was a fine line between documenting the process, and feeling grubby and intrusive. Richard stood right back at the gate and framed his shot wide. After a few knocks and a few minutes of nothingness, the door opened.

Behind it was a woman in her late fifties, neatly dressed and polite. I stood with my hands in front of me and my head dipped, while Shoma explained who we were. I could understand only a few things. I heard *Australia*. And the word for *grandparents*. I heard the word for *father*. And my dad's name. But the rest, I had no idea. Her response was in nods and a series of *I understands*.

And in just those exchanges, knowing very little of what was being said, I knew, without any doubt, that my cousin did in fact still live there and this was his wife, and suddenly I was looking at my relative by marriage. Shoma said a few more things I didn't understand, handed over his business card and started saying goodbye, bowing and saying thank you, so I did the same. We both bowed and said thank you a few more times and left.

'What happened?' I asked him. 'What did she say?'

'It is your cousin's place,' he told me, confirming my thoughts. 'That is his wife. I gave her my business card and asked her to pass it to your cousin, and if he is interested in meeting up, to call me. If he does, we can arrange to meet him.'

Japanese Family

For the days we waited, we kept filming. We went on a walk in the mountains between two old post towns, Tsumago and Magome. They're just two of 69 stops on the Nakasendo Trail, which was used by traders and travellers in ancient times. The towns were places to rest and eat. Now some of them are preserved, looking much like they did hundreds of years ago. I thought of my dad as I walked past a crisp mountain stream and through bamboo forests. I wondered what it had been like for him as a boy in the mountains he called home. I felt him close to me yet far away too.

I went back to Hiroshima and sat in a memorial hall, a beautiful round space so unbearably peaceful. On the walls around me, the city as it became, razed, etched into stone. In the middle of the room was a water sculpture, shaped to represent the time of the bomb, 8:15 am, and the sound of the water trickling around the cool room. Water, for those who died, whose only words in those hours and days afterwards were: *Water. Water. Water.*

But my mind was partly in Tokyo, anxious about my cousin. Anxious that we would hear from him, and what that would mean. Anxious that we would not hear from him, and what that would mean. And, on a train trip from one place to the next, I broke down in tears and told my producer I wanted to go home. It was too much, I said to her. This is my life and it is my story and it is my family and now everyone will know. It feels too raw.

I cried and she just listened. After about ten minutes, she told me that in her experience, this always happens. The person telling their story is enthused at first, they have something to say and they believe in it. But then, as they go along, they feel more exposed, more vulnerable and it can become too much. It happens, she told me. You can go home, but know this is part of the process.

I sat with her words and I sat with my ache and as I looked out the window at trees whizzing by, blurry from the speed of the train, blurry from my tears, I thought of the hundreds of people I had interviewed over the years, who I had asked to tell me their story. The man in jail, his ankle bracelet still on when he came to talk to me. The men who came back from war alive but were barely living. The parents who lost their kids, the kids who lost their parents, the adults who lost their minds.

And the couple whose house turned to ash in an hour, when fires ravaged their community. That day, I was four days into a reporting stint, tired and in the same clothes as the day before that and the day before that and the day before that. I had bought a new phone the previous week and, as I was walking around what was their home, the wife explaining to me that, where you are standing now, that was the front door – I dropped my phone in the ashes of their life and the screen cracked and for a second, a split second, I was annoyed at my clumsiness and at my loss. When I looked back to the wife, she was bent over too. She picked up a necklace, charred and black, and said, 'But we are lucky. We are alive and we have each other and look, here's one of my necklaces.'

They all flashed through my mind on that train and suddenly I knew how it *felt* to be them. I always thanked them for sharing their stories, commended their courage, their honesty, their openness. But I had never really *known*. Not until that moment when I wanted to toss it all in, stomp my foot and get on the next flight home. The vulnerability was excruciating.

But so is hypocrisy. How could I ask them, those whose stories I had built my career on, to do what I wasn't willing to do myself. I turned back to my producer and said, 'OK let's keep going. Let's finish it.'

—

Shoma heard from my cousin within the week while we were still in Hiroshima. He was happy to meet. I decided to make a photo album for him, some sort of way to bridge the 40 years since we last spoke. I found a printing shop on a main street, where trams rolled past, full of life and conversation and colour. A city once beyond dead, now thriving. I didn't have many to choose from, basically whatever was on my phone. Photos of photos. Dad's media press photo, Dad as a teenager with an ancient bow and arrow, Dad and me in the only selfie I ever took of us, drinking coffee, his eyes clouded and old.

Then I went into a bookstore and found a photo album, the cover made of textured paper, red and intricate and dotted with cranes. On the train back to Tokyo, racing past those blurry trees again, I placed the photos in the album. And I sat with the fact I had to do this; there was no going back. And it needed to be filmed.

Tracey and Richard and I talked about that, over coffee and rice balls and green tea in a can. How much would we film? How was it going to unfold? My cousin would meet us after work, but we didn't have a specific time. The plan was to get to the neighbourhood early, sit in a cafe and wait until he called. Would we film that? Would we film us meeting? What about when I tell him how Dad died? How much of that did he need to know? What I did know was that I did not want the camera in the house when I was telling him of Dad's death. I would be filmed going in, taking off my shoes, bowing, and saying hello and thank you. And later, maybe, the camera could come in.

But the in-between bit, the real-life bit, well, some things are better left private, no?

And so, on a dark evening, Shoma and I sat in a coffee shop nearby where my grandparents used to live, and we ordered a tea and marvelled at the hand-drawn menu. And after about an hour, my cousin called and told us he was ready. We paid for our coffees and walked out into the night and around two corners. Richard was there, standing far enough away not to be intrusive, and Tracey, who just days earlier I had told I wanted to go home.

And then we saw a man standing on the street who I didn't recognise but seemed to perhaps recognise me, and I realised it was my cousin. He was shorter than I remembered, and of course older, but something about his smile was familiar. Broad and welcoming. And in my Aussie way, I walked towards him and reached out my arms to give him a hug. At the last minute realised I was in Japan and Australian Kumi was a bit too forward and a bit too familiar, so I retreated into Japanese Kumi and pulled my arms back by my sides and just said, 'Hello, thank you for meeting me,' and bowed.

We walked together towards what had been my grandparents' home, now my cousin's, with Taguchi written on the gate. We walked inside, I took off my shoes and we shut the door on the camera. From there, it was just me and Shoma. My cousin showed us upstairs into a sitting room.

The outside of the house was pretty much the same, but the inside was nothing like it had been. The rooms were smaller and more modern; the large living area I could picture in my mind was no longer. There seemed to be more walls. Or maybe there were always walls, and when I was small everything felt bigger. We sat down and my cousin's daughter came into the room as well. She was about 12 or 13 and smiled a lot, and I thought, what a strange school night for her, this haafu from Australia, her dad's cousin, and random strangers, come to tell her dad about the death of a man she may never have heard about.

I was younger than you, I wanted to tell her, when I played in this house. Your great-grandmother would serve me tea and biscuits and your great-grandfather would sit and smoke and smile and there was a rabbit that was blind in one eye. And I wanted to tell her that her great-grandfather used to own a hardware store and her grandfather – well, did she know about him?

But I just sat there and smiled at her and she seemed happy and that made me happy. I thought that my cousin seemed like a good dad to her. And then her mum came in, the woman who had opened the door to us a few days earlier, and she brought us tea and biscuits and she seemed kind as well. I wished I could tell my dad, 'This is a good family. They seem happy.'

After some thank yous, I started telling them why I was there. Every few sentences I stopped so that Shoma could translate. 'Thank you for having me in your home. I remember this place as a child. I remember us driving around the streets in your car. I came to tell you that Akira died a few years ago and I am sorry I haven't been able to tell you until now. He died in his home. He had been getting old, but he loved where he lived and he played golf and lawn bowls and had a happy life. Here, I made a photo album for you.'

My cousin told me that he remembered us visiting, and that while he had kept in contact with Dad on and off, he hadn't known Dad had died. He said he was happy that Dad had had a good life and that he knew he had been proud of us, his daughters. I said thank you. It was all nice, but it was formal and strange, and then I told my cousin that I wasn't sure what to do because Dad had said he wanted his ashes to stay in Australia, but I wanted to know what he thought of that.

This is not what you do, is it. Dad had expressed his wishes in his will, and I was going to honour them, but it also didn't feel right that no part of him would be in Japan, near his home, with his parents, his family. My cousin paused and said, if that is what Dad had wanted, then it seemed right. So we left it at that. Dad would never come back to where he was born.

I am not sure what I wanted, but I wanted something more. That my dad was cared for and missed. That he would be remembered. I don't know. In that moment, my sister and I were all that Dad had, and he was in Australia in ashes now and I was in his childhood home but it was not the same anymore and my heart ached for some certainty I never knew it needed.

After that, and a bit more chat, I sensed it was time to leave. I knew my cousin would never ask me to go, but it just felt right to end our time together. I started saying thank you for having us and thank you for your time and thank you for the tea, and we all stood. We walked down the stairs, put our shoes on and said goodbye again at the door. And at the last minute, I asked, Shall we have a photo together? So we did. My cousin, his daughter and me. My family. All Taguchis. No arms around each other, no hugs. Formal and polite.

When we drove away, I asked Shoma how he thought it went. I can't tell, I told him. Were they happy to see me? Were we too intrusive? Was the photo album too much? No, he said, I think they are really happy you came. They are? I asked him. Yes, he said. I am sure if you wanted to see them again, they would welcome you.

I believed him. I still do, but I had imagined other scenes. I wanted to share stories of my obaasan and ojiisan. I wanted to hear stories about my dad when he was younger. I wanted to hear more about me when I was small. I wanted to talk about that car ride around the streets and the blind-in-one-eye rabbit. I wanted there to be laughter. I wanted there to be hugs, and 'we are so happy we are in touch'. I wanted there to be phone numbers exchanged, and jokes about how that wouldn't make much difference as our Japanese/English were as bad as each other, and I wanted to share what a great time this was.

That's not how it was, though, and I didn't tell Shoma how sad I felt. I just thanked him, and said I was glad it had gone well, and it was nice to know I had family in Japan. Yet underneath, that family felt even more distant than when I thought I would never see them again.

Still Missing

I miss my dad. One moment everything is fine and the next, I feel a sadness, deep and painful and raw. This time, it comes as I stand in the kitchen, waiting for a pot of water to boil. I am scrolling through photos on my phone, and I see one of my dad where he is probably in his late thirties, so around the late 1960s or early 1970s. He is holding up a camera, I can't see the make but I think it is a Minolta or a Canon. In the black and white photo, Dad is checking a setting and flung over his shoulder is another camera. Maybe this day the feelings have come flooding back because I have been trying to get an old film camera up and running. I bought an old one from eBay Japan, a Canon AE1, which was made around the time I was born. I love the look of it and feel of it and for the past week, I have been finding ways to fit a battery inside and bought a leather strap so I can fling it around my shoulder; finally, today, I got everything I needed. And I see the photo of my dad and his camera and somehow the remembering makes the missing more raw and more tender because I realise there is so much I forget.

In these moments of missing, I think of the photo that led to astronaut Michael Collins being called the world's loneliest man because in 1969 he flew Apollo 11 around the dark side of the moon alone, while his crewmates were landing on it, and lost contact with Earth for over 40 minutes. And I think of the photo he took of the lunar module, housing Neil Armstrong and Buzz Aldrin, in between him and Earth, and at that moment, every single human being bar him, was in that photo.

I think of astronomer Carl Sagan and his pale blue dot. In his 1994 book with the same title, he reflected on an image taken by the Voyager 1 space probe as it moved away from home, towards the edges of our solar system. In that image, Earth is but a tiny speck. He told us how it was our home and always has been. All the joy and all the suffering and all the heroes and all the cowards and all the lovers and teachers and leaders and superstars – all calling this pale blue dot home and how that dot, when zoomed out, looks like a mote of dust in a sunbeam.

Somehow it all feels connected to my missing and that photo of my dad, and I realise that this missing is part of me and I don't want to lose touch with it because in this sadness is my meaning and in this ache is a sorrow that is colourful and beautiful and real and tender.

–

Linda tells me one day that her dad is dying and he doesn't have long left. He had been sick for a while but his decline has been rapid. It's irreversible. She is hurriedly making plans to fly back to see him. She'll bring her baby, a little girl, the one who was in her tummy a year before and survived when a drunk driver ploughed into the side of their car. Now that baby is nearly six months old and has a name. She is earth-side and smiling. In our usual routine of voice messages, Linda and I talk about the strangeness of her life right now: how at the same time as she is nurturing a new life, she is saying goodbye to an old one. I tell her I am so, so sorry.

She tells me that she is not sure what state her dad will be in when she walks into his hospital room, and that she thought she would have more time with him. Then, she says she is not even sure he will be alive when she lands. I tell her I have heard that the dying hang on until they can see all the people they need to see, before they go. And, in the way we do because we know each other so well and care that we each live our best possible lives, I share that I am worried she will try to be too strong. To reassure her dad. *It is OK to cry, Dumpy. You are losing your dad and that is real and it is so terribly sad.*

And then I tell her that he won the lottery, having a daughter like her.

—

My granny once told me that if she ever came back as something, she'd like to come back as a bird so she could fly and be free and soar above the earth. I think of that sometimes when I see a bird and hope that one of them is her and sometimes I feel like she is with me and she is guiding me and I listen.

—

I had a test come back that wasn't great. The test all women dread where our dignity is put on a cold bed in a doctor's office and our legs are spread and the most intimate part of our body is spread open with the help of cold metal tongs and our insides are scraped. And it is uncomfortable and basically shit and we all dread it and all do whatever we can to avoid it, but the reminder notices come and we take a deep breath and tell ourselves it'll be over in 15 minutes. And after it is done, we pull up our underwear and we go back to work and get on with our lives.

The results told me that some cells were not quite right and they told me to come back a year later and do the test again. The next time the cells were not quite right so I jumped online and searched for signs of cervical cancer and signs of ovarian cancer and on every list I ticked at least half the boxes. Even though I knew I was being paranoid, something in me started to believe that maybe, maybe this was true.

I slept badly over a few nights. I would go to bed telling myself it was nothing, as per what I had read on the internet – most likely nothing to worry about, symptoms similar to those of your regular cycle, blah blah – but at that middle-of-the-night time, my brain and body told me differently. I would wake and think, no, this might be it. I would imagine the doctor telling me the news and I would imagine how I would react and I would wonder who I would tell first and how and when.

Then, in those haunting hours, I would start thinking of all that I would miss. My daughter and my cat and my home and the sunshine and the plants on the windowsill and fresh sheets on my bed and the blue sky and boiling the kettle and choosing a cup for my tea. My books and the sunlight in the leaves in the tree outside the window in the late afternoon. And the flowers in spring and my car that always starts and a little toy sheep a friend rescued for me from a shop window.

I would wonder what would happen to all my things and who would have to pack them up, and I would wonder whether my cat who was rescued would know if I died or whether he would think I had abandoned him, and that thought would make me not just cry but sob with a depth of sadness totally out of proportion to my imagined illness.

I would think about the people I would miss and how they would miss me, and I sobbed in advance for my loss and their loss and all that would not be shared and all that would be taken away and all that could have been. And I sobbed for a reality that had not happened but felt so real.

It was as if I was living a story I had heard recounted by many Buddhist teachers, of a monk who said that the cup he held was so precious because in his mind it was already broken and so every time he held it, he appreciated it because he had one more moment with it – for it was never going to last.

–

Here's the thing about narratives. They can become true or at least feel true. With every broken heart and packed box and every house that was dismantled and a new one put together with the help of flat-packed furniture deliveries and allen keys, with every photo of a time either accepted or deleted to insure against further pain, a story would play in my head without me even realising it: I do life better on my own.

Translation: life is painful.

After all, this is who I am, I would tell myself. And, honestly, the version of this book from six years ago said exactly that. I had a theory back then about my first month of life, the one in a humidicrib: that my initial grasp of the world was alone. The sounds and smells of life were experienced from inside a perspex box with controlled heating. That peace and survival was ingrained in my brain to be solo, boxed away.

And so that belief became the story I told myself, and I suppose it was from a place of fear – that maybe that was true and maybe I didn't have what it took to do adult life and hey, that wasn't really my fault because I was wired that way from birth.

—

Sara asked me one day over the phone, What's going to happen if you keep believing the same thing? Our regular Wednesday night chat, her driving home, me sitting in the hallway at home drinking a cup of tea, grappling over some quandary. This time, it was a feeling that I was stuck in old ways of thinking, with anxiety ruling the day. I told her that I was tired of it, tired of my brain telling me stories that weren't true.

What if I keep believing the same thing? I repeated to her. I'm not sure.

You're going to get the same results, she replied. And how has that gone for you so far?

Letting Go

Every few years I would try to find Alexei. I would email Kim and ask her – have you seen him? Do you know where he might be? No, she would tell me, I have lost touch with those guys. And I would find the website of their rescue service and scroll through the rudimentary pages, hoping to see his face somewhere. But he was never there, and I would go through my photos of that time in Moscow and the only photo I had of him was the one of us three together at the airport, backlit, dark. He was a shadow in my mind, and he followed me around, and when I turned around he was there, but I couldn't grasp him.

Follow the logic, a well-known TV host would say, which I took on board as a journalistic lesson many years later. Follow the logic, follow the money – in the case of Alexei, what was the end game, really? Even if I found him, what would I do? Tell him I wanted to bring him to Australia? Send him and his grandmother money? What?

I think I just wanted to help him. That maybe if I found him, I could feel whole again; I had that yearning for meaning and that yearning for my heart to be broken open and that yearning that in him and in his scars and in his kind eyes, there was some answer that I needed.

I needed him more than he needed me and after a few years I gave up looking, but I would notice the moments I wanted to find him again. When life felt hard. When I felt lost. When I felt sad. When I felt disconnected. I needed that ache to make me feel alive, to re-centre me, to ground me back in a place I had forgotten.

–

Recently, I imagined I was walking up a mountain when the night is at its darkest and the stars are bright and beckoning. I got so high on that mountain I could reach my hand up into the sky and touch the stars and feel their warmth. It felt like I was flying there, just like the little girl in the green dress. I was so close to her stars, I could hear them brush up against each other as my fingers pulled through their light, creating music only I could hear.

I held my hand there for a while and her little hand appeared from above me. It reached down and held mine and I held hers. She was so close I could see a small shell button on the sleeve of her green dress, delicate and pretty. Time swirled around and for a moment – or was it many moments – there was nothing.

Without words, she comforted me and I comforted her. It was known and beautiful and temporary. A part of me wanted to stay there but I knew she must stay in her stars and I knew I must walk down my mountain. After a while our hands disconnected. We turned away from each other and we each felt an ache that must be felt. About halfway down, I looked up into the sky and searched for her. I couldn't see her but I asked her anyway, Will I see you again? And there was silence and it was lonely and empty but it felt necessary and right.

All I heard was the wind weaving its way around me and in that wind I heard a voice – no, that is not right – in the wind, I sensed a voice – a voice in my heart that had no sound but the words were so clear: *You're going to be OK.*

An Apartment in Paris

Paris, October 2024. I am here for two weeks.

I am not quite living above a bakery but there is one opposite my building. Outside the kitchen window I can see rooftops and those Parisian buildings, and at night, I watch the traffic come and go through the intersection below.

One evening, a thunderstorm cracks above the city. I open the window even though it's cold, and I watch reflections on the shiny street below. I listen to the raindrops caress the roof. I make a pot of tea and I hold my hands around the cup and I watch the rain some more.

It is quiet. I speak to no-one, apart from a few shopkeepers and I apologise that I have little French. I buy groceries and stock the small fridge with eggs and cheese and yoghurt. There is a wooden chopping board on the bench. On it I place two tomatoes, sun-ripened. One is yellow and one is red, and one night I make a simple omelette and sit at the bench and eat it with salad greens.

I am here, I tell myself. Not just here in Paris, but here – a dream that has been in my head, a picture, an image of an apartment and a city and a feeling. And somehow I have made my way to that image and I have joined a future I saw in my mind, and so much of it is as I imagined.

And because of that, because it has been in my head for so long, I wonder whether I am excited enough. Or another way of putting it: why I am not so elated to be here? Don't get me wrong; I am so happy I am here. But something feels off. I leave voice messages across time zones to my lifelines in this world: Why does this feel normal? I ask them. Does it mean something is wrong? Even on the way here, where the endless hours in the sky mashed together what was and what will be – all that felt normal, too. I don't feel like I am escaping anything, I tell them. Maybe that's what's different.

—

I had been building up to this feeling. In the month or so before I left, I was walking to a Muay Thai class and I felt so damn happy. Walking up my street near my home in Sydney, through what was now my neighbourhood. Walking to a class that was now a community. I left a voice message to Amelia: I am off to my happy place. And then I said to her, Actually, how strange is that. I realise that I have many happy places now.

I had my home, with my pot plants on the windowsill and a linen cupboard full of clean sheets and towels. I had my car, reliable and safe. A healthy daughter, thriving in her adult life. A cheeky, adored cat. A workplace that I found stimulating and meaningful. Loyal friends, and exciting new friendships. There was rarely a space that dragged me down.

Maybe that is why Paris doesn't feel so dramatic, I tell my friends and I tell myself. It just is. No need to shapeshift, no need to be anyone else.

—

On my second day in Paris, I walked back home along a new road, wanting to explore as many unknown streets as possible. As I scanned the map, the name of a theatre popped up. My heart sank. How had I not thought of this until now?

It was that theatre, where concertgoers had been gunned down by men with automatic rifles, with no reason behind who died and who survived. It was a story back then, that story where I saw the alleyway and the man trying to run for his life on a broken foot, and where I told the rest of the newsroom not to watch the video because it would stay in their minds forever.

And now, nearly ten years later, I was at that theatre. A real building on a real street. The theatre looked like it had closed down, lifeless from the day of the shooting onwards. But then I realised it was a Sunday and day time and there were no concerts on.

Even so, the facade had a heavy look about it. I took a photo of it from the other side of the road. There was a couple next to me at the crossing and I felt self-conscious, like I was part of some trauma porn. It's not that, I wanted to tell them. I am here for a reason. Still, it didn't feel good.

As I looked at the lettering on the facade and the name I knew so well – Bataclan – I thought about what I saw that night on screens. The ambulances and the chaos and the bodies covered with sheets. There was a feeling here, sad and violent and grim.

I walked across the road and found a plaque on the wall. *To the victims of the massacre*, it said. There was only one alleyway and I turned down it and I knew it. It was what I saw. It was what I remembered. It was what my brain wouldn't let me forget.

I looked up and saw the windows and wondered which window was the one the man jumped down from. I closed my eyes and I could see the man running as if it was happening now, right now. And I could feel the fear and the sadness. The time in between then and now was pushed together, and it all became one moment. My heart ached and I felt like I had been given a chance to tend to a wound.

—

In Paris, I am time travelling. When I wake up, it's evening in Sydney and Amelia has lived my day already. Linda will be asleep in LA, around midnight, but she is behind me now. And I keep an eye on Bali, too. There, it is mid-afternoon. A man who is on my mind is on holiday. We flew out of Sydney on the same morning, trips planned way before we started chatting at a party a few months before.

I think of him when I wake and when I wander around. Small things remind me of him and most days we share photos of our respective adventures. It is early days but . . . there is something. A sense that he may become part of a future I am yet to know. I am curious. I want to know more about him. And I wonder whether a lifetime will be enough.

—

I have lists of things to see and do, given to me by friends before I left. I do none of them. I just wake up and decide what I feel like from one day to the next. It is liberating and empowering, and gives me space to let life unfold in the way it is meant to. I become acutely aware of that feeling of past and present merging, of moments that I am meant to take note of, ones I must remember.

For example, when I am in Paris, my favourite tennis player, Rafael Nadal, announces his retirement. Rafa, who I had watched in his earliest matches as he conquered the red dirt of Roland Garros, his Parisian home.

Strangely, just a few days before he told the world he was stopping, I had bought a poster of that famous court: a simple green tree, and at the end of each branch, tennis balls, not apples. And, written underneath, in vibrant red letters: *Roland Garros 2011*. Rafa won that one.

My brain likes these synergies. They show me that I am meant to be in this city at this time.

—

There is a day, though, where I feel that missing for a life that never was. A childlike ache. I don't want it to return; I thought I was done with that now. But it has crept back in, a tunnel that runs deep and travels back to a place I forget and cannot reach, and even if I could, there is nothing to hold on to there. I can't touch it or comfort it.

In the shower, I cry. I hold my head in my hands and I have a conversation with her in my head. That little girl in a green dress, floating around the sky. I ask her to come down for a visit, just one more time. I want to walk the streets with her and hold her hand. I want to show her things and get excited about sweet moments together. I want to reassure her and for her to reassure me.

I close my eyes and I picture her floating down and joining me, her bare feet touching the earth. And I weep for losses I cannot explain and a comfort I sometimes cannot find, except through imagining I can go back to there, wherever 'there' is.

—

On another day, I read that a group of Japanese atomic bomb survivors have won the Nobel Peace Prize – a grassroots organisation called Nihon Hidankyo, made up of those who lived beyond Hiroshima and Nagasaki. They've been recognised for their work to abolish nuclear weapons. It feels significant. Over the last ten years, I have written articles about that time, and articles about my dad and his experiences in the war. It has been a focus of my work. I think about a story I was meant to tell, just as the world shut down for years. A trip, long planned, to Nagasaki, where I was going to document the story of 24 Australian prisoners of war, who survived the bomb there. Some of those men had experienced the horror of the Thai–Burma Railway, others were on board a ship when it was sunk by an allied missile. Those men were picked up by the Japanese and worked as slaves. I never got the chance to work on that project and time moved on.

But in the way that it has been in so far, there is something circular, something relevant, in that peace prize being announced: that not all is forgotten and of all the things we must remember, surely the memory of a weapon that can turn bodies into shadows in a split second must become ingrained and imprinted in all minds, in this life and all lives to come.

—

Another day, I go for a slow run to a park just near where I am staying. It is hilly and beautiful and you can see across the city. I wind up and down small paths, much like I did, and do, at that garden in Tokyo. I find a little stream and patches of wildflowers, left to grow as they will. A group of young school children walks past me in a line, out for an adventure they may never remember.

Around another bend, I come across a perfectly grassed hill, one of the ones you would roll down as a kid. It's lush and at the perfect incline, high enough to get some momentum, and long enough to belly-laugh many times. I am tempted to give it a try but the grass is a bit wet. On another day I might. And then, I remember Jenny, a counsellor I had a few years ago.

During one session, we were speaking of joy and laughter and spontaneity – and how, at that time, those vital life forces were so hard to come by – and she asked me: How long has it been since you've swung on a swing? Then, it had been a long time. But now, I want to tell her, many times since. And how I have leaped up and down gutters, and danced for no reason in the streets, and I have hugged and laughed and loved more often than not.

—

On my last day, all I want to do is walk and soak up the city I have come to know. Streets that were unfamiliar, now familiar. I have two strange things I want to do: the first, to find a street and a restaurant that I saw in an episode of a series I have been re-watching, *The Diplomat.*

In one scene, two of the main characters are eating in a bistro. I had forgotten about these scenes in Paris and the city looks magical. I am here right now, I want to tell those characters through the screen. Instead, I take a photo and I zoom in and find the street name and I mark it on my maps as a place to go to.

The other stop I want to make is to a clothes shop I always visit when I am here. I know I will hesitate in spending money but I also know, when I am back home and I see a sweater folded in my drawer or a shirt hanging in my cupboard, I will be reminded of this time. And, more importantly, symbols of a promise to myself, that I kept.

So, I walk through the cold grey city and I try to take every moment in. And when my mind races to yesterday or to tomorrow, or to a to-do list after a day or two in the skies, I urge it back to now. *You may never be here again*, I tell myself. *We don't know how many years we have for our lives.*

I find the street and I find the bistro and I take a photo, fiction and non-fiction merging. Then I walk to the shop I love and I buy a shirt that feels beautiful and a colourful cardigan that makes me smile. A delicate bracelet and a matching pair of earrings.

I text Amelia and Linda and send them photos of the shop and what I have bought, and I feel their excitement from across time.

Then, I take the metro back to my apartment. I pack and organise my things and get ready for an early start. I wipe the benches and take the rubbish down the lift to the courtyard. I read and I write. And I make a pot of tea and watch a movie called *Lonely Planet*. It's about a writer and she is on a deadline to finish her book, so she holes up at a retreat in Morocco.

There, she connects with a man (younger than her but, thankfully, barely mentioned), and they fall in love and it's a story not about age-gap relationships, but about the best form of love: of two people meeting, their lives not necessarily all tidy, but, for some reason, each truly sees the other and likes who they are. Simple. Beautiful.

And as I watch, I think of all the other things I should have done but didn't. The bakeries and clothes shops and bistros and music bars. But I feel no guilt. This trip had to unfold in its own way – where days would become what they wished, and, like a dance, Paris and I paired up and created our own world.

–

That evening, I walk downstairs and eat at the bistro on the corner. A simple salad. A cheese plate. A glass of crisp white. I sit on the sidewalk and watch the world go by. A man walks past me, tearing a chunk off the end of a baguette. A father slings his son over his shoulder like a satchel. A young couple holds hands and I wonder what their story is. I write in my notebook and sip my wine and avoid looking at my phone. All that is in there can wait.

As I eat, I sense a figure standing next to me, and then I hear a hello. I look up and it is David.

Earlier in the week, I had eaten dinner at a bistro a bit further up the road. I sat in the window and ordered what seemed to be the most-recommended dish. The chicken mafé – a peanut-based stew, from Senegal. It had been incredible – one of the best meals I have ever had. And I met the chef, David, who had lived in Paris for decades. I'd contemplated going back there for my final dinner but wanted to stay close to home. And now David walks past me on his way to work. He's dressed in a smart jacket and shirt, and is carrying an umbrella in case it rains. He asks me how I am, and I tell him I am great (true). I ask him how he is and he says he is great (true, I am sure). And then he tells me that the bistro I am eating at is the first business he owned, many years ago. No way, I say. Yes, he smiles again.

I tell him how nice it is to see him again, and that I hope I will see him soon. But I don't tell him I am leaving in the morning. I am not quite ready to accept that I may not have that chicken mafé again. And I don't want him to think I didn't spend my last meal in his current bistro up the road – his loving tribute to a family, and a home, across the seas.

—

When I go back upstairs, I take a photo of the last sunset from the arched bedroom window. The sky glows orange and the rooftops fade. My travel clothes are laid out, ready for the early alarm and train to the airport. I am ready to go home. I want to go home. I am excited about all that is to come.

And as I drift off to sleep in what was once just a Parisian dream, I wonder which memories I will remember and which memories I will forget. And I wonder which will swirl back to me in years to come when I least expect them, making their own way back to me through time. I wonder, too, what they will come to mean.

All I know is that some will return, but that is for days yet to come. For now, they can rest.

Acknowledgements

It took me years longer to write this than I anticipated. Thank you to Dan Ruffino and Simon & Schuster for your patience, to my editors, Michelle Swainson and Jo Lyons – and to my publisher, Ben Ball, who understood me from the beginning and cared about this book as if it were his own.

I am indebted to author Sarah Sentilles, the only person I could trust with my first draft, and whose wisdom and guidance have helped me beyond measure.

The seeds of this book were planted in 2015, when I wrote a piece on the 70th anniversary of the Hiroshima atomic bomb. Thank you to the Australian Broadcasting Corporation and *Meanjin* for seeing the value in my words.

Two years after that, I was invited onto one of Australia's most-known radio shows and podcasts, *Conversations*. Special thanks to Richard Fidler for providing a safe space, and for making me consider there might be a story to tell.

In 2018, I signed with Simon & Schuster, and in 2019, I filmed a documentary in Japan around similar childhood themes. Deep gratitude to Jessica Douglas-Henry, Tracey Spring and Richard Corfield; and to Melanie Brock and Shoma Brock.

I speak about people in this book who have shaped me. Some are living, some are not, some I am not sure. It is hard to say thank you for their stories because so many have come from hardship and pain. But, thank you, Pauline and Daniel, for supporting me in sharing Scott's story. He will always be remembered.

Finally, love to: my family, Ryan, Sara, Linda, Amelia, Bug and Coco.

About the Author

Born in Melbourne, Victoria to her Japanese father and Australian mother, Kumi Taguchi grew up in rural New South Wales learning classical violin from the age of five. She has worked in the media for over 25 years in Australia and overseas, and is currently the host of SBS's *Insight*.